Soul-Hearted LIVING

A Year of Sacred Reflections & Affirmations for Women

DR. DEBRA REBLE

InspiredLIVING PUBLISHING

A SACRED GIFT FROM MY HEART TO YOURS!

4-Part
Soul-Hearted LIVING
Sacred Meditation Series

You'll receive the following meditations:

- Opening Your Heart to Your Authentic Self
- Tapping into Your Inner Wisdom
- Awakening to Your Divine Essence Within
- The Five-Minute Heart-Opener for the Busy Woman

DOWNLOAD YOUR SACRED GIFT SET TODAY AT:

http://bit.ly/SHLGiftSet

Published by Inspired Living Publishing, LLC.
P.O. Box 1149, Lakeville, MA 02347

Requests to publisher for permission should be addressed to the Permissions Department, Inspired Living Publishing, P.O. Box 1149, Lakeville, MA 02347 or by e-mail at Linda@InspiredLivingPublishing.com.

ISBN-13: 978-1-7327425-2-9
ISBN-10: 1-7327425-2-9
Library of Congress Control Number: 2018964672

Cover and Layout Design: Mandy Gates, MandyGates.com
Editor: Deborah Kevin, DeborahKevin.com

Printed in the United States.

DEDICATION

This book is dedicated to...

Every woman who yearns to courageously embrace her truth, step into her authentic power, and be true to her soul's path.

Every woman who says yes to shining her light and illuminating the path for other women to follow so they know they are not alone on their journey.

And also to. . .

Special colleagues, mentors, friends, and family members who have been instrumental in making this book a reality, including:

Linda Joy, my soul-hearted friend, mentor, and publisher, whose spiritual guidance and loving support have created the sacred container for this book to be birthed into the world. Thank you for helping me see my light and fulfill my soul's calling as a spiritual leader of love. You saw my soul potential when I couldn't see it for myself and it has made all the difference.

Deborah Kevin, whose loving encouragement and editorial vision elevated this book to be more than I could have imagined.

Mandy Gates, who brought the concept of Soul-Hearted Living to life on the cover and interior of this book through her visionary artistry.

Charlotte Bifulco, my dear soul friend who helped me edit each passage before I sent them off to my editor and lovingly encouraged me when I doubted myself.

Debbie Sain-Bissette, my longtime soul friend, who created sacred space for me to write and for being one of my best cheerleaders.

To all the fearless female visionaries who embraced their truth and stepped into their light by gracing this inspirational project with their original quotes. Thank you for believing in your divine wisdom and sharing it with the world. Your light has inspired me to shine even brighter.

The multitude of extraordinary clients, whose dedication to spiritual transformation, inner soul work, and life-changing results inspired me to develop this material.

My dear friends, the rare gems in my life, who have come into my life for a reason, season, or lifetime, and who stand by me with their patience, encouragement, and unending support.

With infinite love, joy, and gratitude to the hearts of my heart: my son, Tom and my daughter, Alex. Your radiant light, beautiful souls, and loving energies have facilitated my own transformation and inspired me to be a better person. I'm blessed and honored that you were gifted to me in this lifetime.

My precious grandson, Elliot who lights up my world and has captured my heart. May you always express the divine essence of love that you are.

My father, a blessing in my life. Without you, I would not be who I am today. Thank you for encouraging me to follow my heart. My dear husband, best friend, love of my life, and soul-hearted partner, Doug, who believed in me even when I stopped believing in myself. Thank you for your loving support to create my dreams and fulfill my sacred soul's purpose. I love you with all my heart.

And finally, you, the reader, the beautiful woman whose essence is love. Thank you for coming home to your heart and heeding the call of your soul. It is an honor to guide you on your soul's path. May these words spark truth in your heart that resonates with your soul, and may they empower you to live an inspired and fulfilled life.

INTRODUCTION

We all have powerful intuitive moments when we channel information that comes directly from our divine source. These divine downloads are when our heart expands, time stands still, and we tap into the essence of our soul. The idea of soul-hearted living revealed itself to me in one of these awe-inspired moments of spiritual clarity.

Twelve years ago, I was in the midst of writing my first book which would eventually become Soul-Hearted Partnership. I was sitting at my desk doodling on a notepad, taking a well-needed creative break from the manuscript. While doodling, I dropped into my heart space, tranced out for a few moments, and tapped into my divine source.

This divine connection was affirmed when I felt a rush of goosebumps or what I call "God bumps" move through me. In that inspired moment, I received a divine download and wrote the word, "Soul-Hearted" on the pad. I knew that Soul-Hearted Living was what I was meant to birth to the world. Since then, I have fine-tuned the spiritual principles of soul-hearted living during workshops, retreats, and thousands of individual consultations so that they can easily be incorporated into everyday life.

So, what does it mean to live a soul-hearted life?

Soul-Hearted Living is a call to come home to your heart and live in alignment with your soul's journey. What I refer to as soul-hearted is a flow of soul energy channeled through your heart and expressed through your human experience. It's living aligned with your heart and soul and being true to this path in your life.

Living soul-heartedly nurtures positive energy, vitality, and optimism. When you co-create what you want in alignment with what is best for yourself, others, and the world, this flow becomes a spiritual path that leads to living peacefully, joyfully, and abundantly. It's a sacred path of viewing life as the gift it is—despite its challenges.

The teachings of *Soul-Hearted Living* consist of heart-centered practices to support you in waking in the morning intending, affirming, and walking in grace every day.

What I've discovered on my own soul-hearted path, as well as working with clients for over two decades, is that when we make discerning choices inspired by love instead of fear, we become co-creators of our lives in sync with our soul's journey. We choose what soulfully aligns with us, and what does not. We make conscious choices that not only sustain our well-being, but also the well-being of the planet and all its inhabitants. Each enlightened choice we make from our hearts serves ourselves as well as others' highest and greatest good.

The *Soul-Hearted Living* book features a daily reflection, an inspirational quote, and an affirmation. There's no right or wrong way to read this book. You can choose to start from the beginning of the book or today's date, or flip the pages to intuitively chose the message that's meant for you. You can also journal on the message of the day to dive deeper into its meaning.

Throughout *Soul-Hearted Living*, you'll discover original inspirational quotes from women in my sacred community as well as leading luminaries. I believe that all women have an innate wisdom that, when shared, has the power to inspire, empower, and support other women on the path.

My deepest desire in writing this book is that you remember the truth of who you are, allow your authentic self to lead the way, trust in the wisdom of your heart, follow love over fear, and that you give yourself permission to shine so bright that you become a beacon of love and light for others.

Live a soul-hearted life,

Dr. Debra L. Reble

THE POWER OF CHOICE

"It is through inspired action, baby steps toward our dreams,
that we test the mettle of our convictions, and show
the Universe that we mean business."

– BRYNA HAYNES

The quality of your life is determined by the choices you make in every moment. It's a new year and a perfect time to make inspired choices in alignment with your soul's journey.

Choice is a powerful tool when you understand, on a soul level, that you are accountable for your life. It's always your choice how you express your soul's energy and how you experience this expansive energy flow in your everyday life.

The more impeccable and discerning your choices are using this energy, the more you will experience physical, emotional, and spiritual well-being. Today, take one inspired action toward fulfilling your dreams.

I make inspired choices based on the wisdom of my soul, not the chatter of my mind.

PERMISSION TO PAUSE

*"Our commitment to our healing is in itself a self-nurturing
act as it allows us to move toward wholeness and
embrace our authentic truth and beauty."*

– KELLEY GRIMES, MSW

When you feel that surge of energy you negatively label as
"anxiety," pause, open your heart, and breathe deeply. Give
yourself the permission to pause so that you can drop into your
heart space and commune with your inner truth.

Once you calm the deluge of thoughts, slow down your
breathing, come into present awareness, and gently remind
yourself that you are confident in your ability to respond to any
challenging situation.

Ask yourself, "What was the trigger of my anxiety? What spiritual
information am I being guided to see? or What is this person or
situation showing me about myself?" Then follow the guidance
of your heart.

I give myself permission to pause
so I can choose to respond to any
challenging situation.

LETTING GO

"The most important thing that matters is spending time with those you love, so surround yourself with those who love, support, and care for you unconditionally."

– DR. DEBRA REBLE

Letting go is one of the most important spiritual principles that you can practice in your life. Too often, you brace yourself for change instead of letting go and embracing change as an opportunity for your personal transformation. When you resist change, you actually generate more energy around your deepest insecurities, drawing toward you what you fear most.

Letting go takes an open heart, expanded awareness, and a willingness to move through fear. Trust in yourself and your connection to source. Like the air you breathe, letting go must become an essential element in your life.

Surrounding yourself with loving people and environments can also support you in releasing what is unnecessary in a healthy and positive way.

I let go of fear and courageously move forward with a peaceful heart.

CONSCIOUS AWARENESS

"When you realize it is not an external incident that causes your pain but your own thoughts about it, you can control how you want to feel."

– MAL DUANE, CPC, CRC

Conscious awareness is what gives way to focused attention. It helps you discern whether you are moving in a flow of positive energy or stuck in the muck and mire of negativity.

Instead of being bound by the chains of negative mindsets and beliefs, you can clear the negativity from your body and mind by replacing them with healthier, enlightened ways of being. You do this by first becoming consciously aware of your thoughts, feelings, and choices.

When you surrender to light as your true state of being, you let go of fear, open to love, and transcend all circumstances no matter how difficult they may seem at the time.

I see, sense, and intuit what is in alignment with my soul's journey.

SOW SEEDS OF LIGHT

"The fires we walk through serve to refine us into the purest of gold. It is through the fire's refining we remember our true purpose."

– CERI RIDENOUR

Let your mantra be to sow seeds of light wherever you go so that you leave it a better place for being there. Shining your light so that others may benefit and follow its path is your constant intention.

As you move through your day, maintain an open heart and express love no matter where you are, who you are with, or what you are doing. Keeping your thoughts nonjudgmental, your words kind, and your choices compassionate, you create universal love and a spiritual attunement with everyone and everything.

I celebrate life, share love, and shine the light of my being.

LOOKING WITHIN

*"Tragedy spares no one; it just courts each of us differently.
It carves a path into our hearts, where grace can greet us."*

– GWENDOLYN M. PLANO

Become intimate with yourself so that you are aware of your imperfections, vulnerabilities, and behavioral patterns and how certain circumstances, people, thoughts, and emotions trigger them.

Practice looking within when you become reactive and see what needs to examined, released, or resolved. It's healthy to pause, sit quietly, and let things surface until you know what's going on within you. Chances are once you're aware of what is really there, it will take care of itself.

I embrace my vulnerabilities
with all my heart.

NAVIGATING TRANSITIONS

"Turn your challenges into blessings. Turn your anxiety into spiritual guidance."

– DR. DEBRA REBLE

Transitions are intense periods of discovery, self-healing, and personal transformation. As such, they are opportunities to let go of what you don't want in your life and co-create what you do want. These are the times for gathering strength in preparation for the next step forward in your life and when used wisely are powerful.

Your intentions, especially when directed consciously, set in motion these transformational shifts. It's up to you to make inspired choices that best utilize this creational energy. These are the times when you know your memo to the universe has been heard, and everything feels as if it is in commotion or "co-motion." Your spirit is bringing in new information to guide this next phase of your life.

I use transitions as
spiritual passages that lead to my
personal transformation.

DIRECTING YOUR ENERGY

"There is something truly liberating about taking yourself off autopilot and making choices from a place of truth in the moment."

– DR. CATHERINE HAYES, CPCC

Sustaining a positive flow of energy is a key to manifesting a happy, fulfilling and peaceful life. It's not just the power of positive thinking that manifests your intentions, it is the flow of energy that you channel positively and productively which creates the quality of your life.

Directing your energy in this way, you co-create what you want in your life. This positive flow becomes a spiritual path that leads to living joyfully, abundantly, and well.

I am accountable for the flow of energy that I bring to every moment.

THE CYCLES OF LIFE

"In the space between our thoughts, we receive the whisper of spirit guiding us through our hearts."

– DR. DEBRA REBLE

In the natural world, cycles, such as the changing seasons, the rings of trees, and the spiral of shells, perpetuate life and reflect transformation. These cycles govern cosmic rhythms. Having an awareness of participating in life's cyclical transformations affords you a spiritual clarity that promotes healing and a sense of wholeness.

By observing these natural rhythms, you can attune to your own spiritual growth. An amazing sense of peace comes with knowing that you move through such cycles throughout your life and every transition brings the uncertain and unpredictable opportunity for change.

I move through the cycles of my life with ease and grace.

SLOWING DOWN TO TUNE IN

"Emotions are the glue that connects your spirit to your human form. They can be sticky and uncomfortable as well as joyful and intoxicating."

– CRYSTAL COCKERHAM

Observing yourself as if in slow motion gives you time to become aware of your thoughts, emotions, and sensations. Slowing down your pace moves you into mindfulness where you may notice things you wouldn't have seen before. Being aware of yourself helps you to become more present with what's going on within you, and this is where you have the power to interrupt and, ultimately, release any reaction.

When you are in your heart space, you can consciously observe any thoughts, feelings, or sensations that you are having. In this expanded awareness you can ask yourself: "What is this physical or emotional reaction telling me?" These feelings are trying to get your attention and tell you something. Ask your heart what it is.

I give myself permission to
slow down so I can hear what
my heart is telling me.

EXPRESS GRATITUDE

"Your soul needs time for solitude and self-reflection. In order to love, lead, heal and create you must nourish yourself first."

– LINDA JOY

Begin every day by expressing gratitude for opportunities to open your heart. No matter what your circumstances, daily bless yourself, your fellow human beings, and the earth; then express appreciation for your unique gifts. Gratitude opens your heart and helps you hear the voice of spirit guiding your life.

Expressing gratitude for such spiritual guidance inspires you with the knowledge that you are not alone on your soul journey through life. Being grateful also strengthens your sense of connection with your divine source and the universe.

I wake up every morning with gratitude for what the universe has in store for me.

LIGHTNESS OF HEART

*"Give yourself the permission to pause to
create sacred space—space to consciously choose how
you want to respond to any situation."*

– DR. DEBRA REBLE

You can be light-hearted in every situation no matter how challenging. Keep a sense of humor, playfulness, and silliness when you make a mistake or a mess. Laugh at your yourself when you overcook the turkey, break a favorite vase, or step in a puddle with your good shoes.

Take yourself and life less seriously. Make time to play, have fun, and celebrate "being." In doing so, you will feel more connected, carefree, and present with others.

Being light-hearted naturally liberates the mind, opens the heart, and lifts the spirit. In this state of pure being, you are free to channel your energies happily and live beyond any limitations.

I sustain a lightness of heart no
matter how challenging the situation.

COMFORT ZONES

"Beauty is a feeling, a way of being, a kind of perception, and a method of inspiring others."

– MARIE MARTIN

You may want to remain in your comfort zone and hold on to your protective shell. Such a comfort zone can paralyze you within its limitations. If you don't break free and let go of what keeps you stuck, you will feel cemented in the quicksand of your past. By breaking free, you can move courageously forward and welcome the opportunities that your future holds.

Stepping out of your comfort zone and trusting the current of life to carry you forward brings you to fascinating new shores. So take the first step. One foot after the other. Cross one threshold after another. Take one deep breath at a time.

With courage of heart, I step out
of my comfort zone and
toward my dreams.

OPEN YOUR HEART

"Life is one long experience of practicing. It consists of making mistakes and learning every day. Mistakes are the guideposts to success!"

– KATHLEEN GUBITOSI, MA

Open your heart and be brave enough to reveal yourself to someone. Then, reciprocate and really see that person, too. Sharing your innermost thoughts and feelings with another allows you to forge intimate and meaningful relationships.

When you reveal your true being to another, intimacy bridges any chasm that separates. Although it may be uncomfortable at first, it is emotionally fulfilling to relate to others in such an intimate way. Revealing your authentic self brings you closer together, and your intimate connection gives you a common ground upon which to grow in your relationship spiritually.

I reveal my true self to another open-heartedly and without reservation.

LEAN IN

"Soul connection is a precious gift you give yourself. When in alignment with your soul and living your passions, anything is possible, and miracles happen!"

– KRIS GROTH

Sometimes you may feel frustrated or disappointed when life doesn't go the way you think it should. As a result, you may become rigid and methodical. You may try to micromanage every situation which only makes things worse.

Rather than trying to control the situation through sheer force of will, trust yourself, let go of control, and align yourself with the flow of positive energy that comes through your heart.

Like surfing, if you lean into your experience, breathe deeply, and allow yourself to flow rather than resist, you will be able to move smoothly through any wave without falling off of your board.

I let go of trying to control my life and let it unfold in the best way possible.

REST AND RESTORE

"Seeing yourself as blessed and abundant can shift your perception, ease your anxieties, and create a more positive outlook."

– DR. DEBRA REBLE

Taking sufficient breaks gives your body an opportunity to let go of tension, fatigue, and repair itself. Allow yourself to rest, restore, and let go of your responsibilities. In doing so, you will find that you feel healthier and more at peace.

While your many obligations may compel you to forge ahead, your health and well-being depend on your willingness to listen to your body's cues to slow down, relax, and take breaks. Even taking short breaks in between tasks, spending time in solitude, or engaging in an activity that you enjoy can help release any stress you may experience because of your busy schedule.

I give myself permission to take
a break to rest and restore.

LET GO AND TRUST

"Take time to enjoy your journey. Rest stops, celebrations, and gratitude helps you stay attuned to the essence of your vision."

– ANN SANFELIPPO

Letting go of your negative thoughts, fears and expectations moment to moment brings you into expanded awareness. It takes more than deep breaths and positive mantras to let go; it requires strength of trust and courage of the heart.

Ultimately, you must trust that letting go is about the completion of life cycles and thus, signals a beginning more than an end. You have a choice in every moment to let go into trust.

I choose to let go of fear
and embrace trust.

BE YOUR OWN SOULMATE

"Living in your authentic truth is the gateway to a joyful, freedom-filled life."

– KELLY MISHELL

You may think that there is only one true soulmate for each person and you have to seek out this person to be happy. In reality, however, there are thousands of soul mates with whom you can interact throughout a lifetime.

The relentless search for the one perfect person to complete you is one of the ego's most persuasive delusions. Your spirit doesn't have a vested interest in any one particular person. Many individuals on this earth are here to assist you on your soul's journey. They enhance your life by inspiring insights, unconditional love, and spiritual assistance.

You attract soul-connected people into your life by becoming your own soulmate.

I am whole and complete
and committed to being
my own soulmate.

THE POWER OF INTENTION

"Vulnerability is the pathway to an authentic life."

– DR. DEBRA REBLE

Like an inspired artist facing a blank canvas, you can use intention to alter the course and quality of your life. Intention, when supported by your connection to a divine energy source, sets up the people, places, and opportunities that shape your future realities.

Using the power of intention is not about setting a specific goal and focusing so much on it that you lose sight of other possibilities. On the contrary, it is about being open to the many opportunities that present themselves in manifesting that intent and making the discerning choices most likely to bring about your desired outcome.

I am powerful and have the power
to envision and co-create whatever
my heart desires.

TAKING CARE OF YOU

*"Grow your spiritual soul of authenticity, let go of
the mindset that you must be what others think you
should be and be divinely you!"*

– CINDY HIVELY

Once you become aware that your personal needs are just as
important as those of your family, friends, and coworkers, you
start developing a loving, caregiving relationship with yourself.
By honoring your need for personal time and engaging in
activities that restore and inspire you, you will have more energy
and stamina to serve others energetically.

Make a covenant to be true to yourself. Resolve to pay attention
to your own needs first so that you and your loved ones benefit.

I commit to taking care of my own
spiritual, emotional, and physical
needs first so I can serve others from
my highest vibration.

COMMUNICATING WITH LOVE

"To fall in love is magical; to flow in love is mystical."

– DR. DEBRA REBLE

Listen more responsively and speak less reactively. You will find that your partner or friends will be more open if you respond meaningfully and support their need to be heard.

You can lovingly communicate by taking turns sharing and listening to each other with non-judgment, respect, acceptance, and without interruption.

Be aware of your feelings or desires so that you can articulate them clearly and ask for what you need. Ask yourself, "What am I feeling right now that I need to communicate with this person?" Then pause before sharing so you can speak openly and lovingly from your heart.

I communicate with others from an open and loving heart.

EMBRACING PLAYFULNESS

"Peace, quiet, and time to reflect are priceless, non-negotiable gifts we can give to ourselves. Make unplugging from the day-to-day a priority."

– DEBORAH KEVIN

Being silly, spontaneous, and playful are a few keys to sustaining a positive flow of energy in your life. You may feel inhibited about expressing yourself freely, sensing that society frowns on adults being free-spirited. If you take life too seriously, grow up, and act like an adult, you lose your sense of life being a passionate adventure to be enjoyed and shared.

Children are your best teachers of playfulness because they endlessly infuse light-force energy into their interactions with life. Observe the lightheartedness of a child as they splash in puddles, chase fireflies, build forts, or fairy alters. Tap into your own inner child and do more of the things that make your heart sing.

I allow myself to be playful
and express my inner child.

RELEASING WITH LOVE

*"If there is only one message that I can share and that you
will take to heart, it's this: you are already enough."*

– MICHELLE LEWIS

The practice of letting go is one of the greatest catalysts for
your spiritual growth. When you release anyone or anything, you
open to a flow of divine energy for creative use. Such a release
unleashes energy to support your transformation and a greater
discernment of your choices.

Whether this release feels like a tsunami or a gentle wave, you
are up for life-altering change. You can release whatever isn't in
alignment with your soul's path by trusting yourself and your
connection with source. When you surrender to this energy,
you invite in intense periods of self-discovery, self-healing,
and self-awakening.

I lovingly release anyone or anything
that isn't in alignment with
my soul's path.

SHINE YOUR LIGHT

"It's not enough to just wish and pray. The actions we take MUST align with what we say we want to manifest in our lives for them to appear."

– JESSICA DUGAS

Light energy channeled through your heart is a force that allows you to co-create your own reality. By channeling this energy, you recognize fortuitous circumstances and opportunities as they show up in your life. You become the master of your destiny and direct your energies positively to attract what you want into your life.

It is the light of your being that must shine forth beyond everything—for that is your connection to your divine source and the basis for your full self-expression in life. Be the light, let it flow through your heart, and shine, shine, shine.

The light of my being is
eternal, infinite, and shines brightly,
illuminating my soul's path.

GO WITH THE FLOW

"There are two ways of spreading light. To be the candle or the mirror that reflects it."

– EDITH WHARTON

Flexibility takes a loving acceptance of yourself, others, and the natural ebb and flow of life. You can "go with the flow" and trust that whatever is happening in your life is a spiritual opportunity.

Like a bamboo tree in a storm, flexibility allows you to bend without breaking. It gives you the ability to turn stumbling blocks into stepping stones and problems into opportunities.

To go with the flow, you have to let go of trying to control other people or your current circumstances. This practice helps you stay centered, create peace, and make positive use of any situation.

I accept whatever is happening in my life, make positive use of the situation, and shift it to reflect my highest good.

RADIATE LOVE

*"Embrace the you that has always been there
and introduce her to yourself and your loved ones,
and let her shine through all the layers."*

– JAMI HEARN

Affirm your connection to light energy and soul power on every level. Radiate love through what you think, speak, feel, and act. Think of it as the direct link to your soul. Send out this high-frequency vibration into the world, and the energy you radiate will expand and attract more of the same power in return.

Maintain the circulation of such loving energy through your positive thoughts, feelings, and choices that benefit you as well as the higher good of humanity. Strive to enjoy all the blessings in life and celebrate light energy flowing through you every day.

I am the radiant expression of
love and light energy.

LOVING COMPASSION

"When we at last release the 'heart stuff,' we become whole again."
– DR. DEBRA REBLE

Open your heart in loving compassion for yourself and others and stop getting caught up in the drama of everyday life. Focus your energies on the positive aspects of your life and trust that you can move beyond whatever is blocking your spiritual path. Begin each day by affirming your being, your life, and the value of your experiences. Acknowledge the blessings of who you are and what you already have.

Catch any negative thoughts and release them before they become words or actions. Open your heart and listen to the whisper of spirit as it guides your life in miraculous ways.

I open my heart in loving compassion
to myself and others.

COACH YOURSELF WITH LOVE

*"A miracle is the moment you know that you have
the power to change anything in your life by changing
the meaning that you give it."*

– MICHELE GREER

By becoming your own loving coach, you can respond to any
situation proactively rather than reactively. Open your heart and
project the beauty of your inner being as this will help you see
yourself in a positive light. Mostly, acknowledge that you are
doing the best you can.

Release anything that keeps you stuck in a holding pattern.
Forgive yourself for your past choices and visualize yourself
moving forward and making impeccable choices in the future.
Trust the voice of spirit and eliminate negative thoughts,
replacing them with positive ones.

I lovingly coach myself by using
positive and supportive self-talk.

TAPPING IN

*"To love another is a beautiful gift but to be able
to receive their love is an even greater gift."*

– ISABELLA ROSE

Opening your heart links you to your true being. When you open
your heart, light energy flows through you as pure love, allowing
you to receive and transmit energy that is divinely sourced.
Through your open heart, you channel spiritual information to
guide your life.

You can tap into this energy to lovingly connect with yourself
and others. In this state of open-heartedness, you feel relaxed and
compassionate toward everyone and everything around you. With
this energetic expansion comes a sense of peace, tranquility, and a
spiritual attunement with the universe.

I open my heart and connect to the
source of my true being, which links
me to everyone.

DISENGAGE WITH LOVE

*"There comes a time to move in the world as if you're free
to reclaim your birthright. The time is always now."*

– YAELLE SCHWARCZ

Whenever people come into your life, they often show you
something about yourself that you need to either release
or transform.

When unhealthy people try to hook you into their negativity
or drama, remind yourself that you have the ability to pause,
the power to disengage, and the knowledge of who you truly
are. You can take your focus off the other person and place it
back on yourself. By keeping your attention on your heart, you
can illuminate space, choose to respond positively, and remove
yourself from others' drama.

Change how you respond to any person, and the situation
will change.

I choose to disengage from
negativity and respond positively
to any situation.

THE GIFT OF SOLITUDE

"Our spiritual resilience makes it possible not only to endure hardship and suffering but to use any challenging situation for spiritual growth and transcend even the most devastating circumstances in our lives."

– DR. DEBRA REBLE

Make an effort to nurture a deeper introspective relationship with yourself. It's often difficult to find time in your busy life to spend time alone, be reflective, and listen inwardly. Yet, solitude and reflection open your heart to self-love, expand your awareness, and connect you with your divine source.

Spend time every day in quiet reflection. Walk in nature, sit in a garden, meditate a few minutes each day, soak in a bathtub, or write in a journal. Create a sacred space to commune with yourself as if you were with an old, trusted friend whom you love and accept.

I nurture an introspective relationship with myself by spending time alone.

THE PATH TO HEALING

"It is our choices that show what we truly are,
far more than our abilities."

– J. K. ROWLING

Facing your deepest vulnerabilities is the path to healing yourself and expressing your fullest potential. You may hide behind a wall of protection, afraid that if you let your guard down, let someone in, or let your feelings emerge, you will spiral out of control.

But, when you lean into your deepest fears and insecurities, you are more open to personal transformation than at any other time. In these moments of spiritual awakening, you peel away the hard shell of your ego revealing the divine essence of your own being.

I lean into my vulnerabilities with courage and loving compassion.

TAKING RESPONSIBILITY

"For the first time in a long time, perhaps many lifetimes of waiting, her soul felt her worth. At that moment, she saw that she was and is sacred wealth."

– MARCIA MARINER

Being responsible is being "response-able"—that is, being able to respond rather than react to life's challenges. To co-create the life you want, you have to be responsible for your intentions and the choices you make.

Ask yourself, "Do I take responsibility for my choices and the life I've created?" or "Do I keep making the same choices which bring about the same results?"

Co-creating the life you want begins with you. When you take responsibility for the divine energy that flows through you, you are empowered to envision and co-create whatever you want in your life.

I am responsible for co-creating the life I desire.

 FEBRUARY 3

ALIGN YOUR INTENTIONS

"The brightest lights in our lives shine when we are truly aligned with our destiny and purpose."

– JOYCE FENNELL

Be aware of your thoughts, feelings, and actions and discern if they are directing positive energy into the world. Bless and release all energy not in alignment with the highest and best good of all.

Set your intentions to bring about greater good, peace, and light to all human beings no matter what their circumstances. When your intentions originate from the flow of pure love, they transcend negativity and become a positive force that will transform you and the world.

I align my intentions with the infinite, transformative energy of love.

SHIFTING TIDES

*"Life is a series of births, deaths, and transitions
that ultimately lead to soul-hearted transformation."*

– DR. DEBRA REBLE

It isn't easy navigating the shifting tides of transformation. You may feel ungrounded, unsettled, and question who you are and what you truly want. These feelings bring an opportunity to discover your true self and let go of your ego. Remind yourself to hold steady, open your heart, and trust yourself no matter if you lose your balance, your job, a friend, or family member.

You are in preparation for your future and being given the amazing opportunity to change direction, clear your path of anything that doesn't serve you, and set new intentions of what truly does. So move with ease and grace and trust that your divine plan is unfolding.

When I am at peace, everything
unfolds with ease and grace.

THE ENERGY OF LOVE

"Instant Mood Changer: change your current painful ruminating thoughts to ruminating thoughts of all the many things you ARE doing right."

– MICHELLE DEEB

Love yourself and others passionately, patiently, and without reservation. Practice loving-kindness and non-judgment, especially with yourself. Be open to others' perspectives, offer loving feedback when invited, and speak from your heart. Forgive yourself quickly, and you will find it easier to forgive others.

Pure love alone unites, completes, and fulfills you. Shine your light so that others may benefit. Most of all, celebrate life, express pure love, and sustain the light of your being.

I am the infinite, all-encompassing energy of love in the world.

NAVIGATING RELATIONSHIPS

*"When you feel abandoned, lonely or alone, sit in
silence and allow God to fill the empty space. Your heart
will open to the truth of your perfection!"*

– CARMELLA CALTA

Letting go of a relationship can be challenging especially when that person has been a part of your life for a long time. Yet, not every relationship is supposed to last a lifetime—some are for a reason, a season, or a lifetime.

By letting go of the relationships that no longer aligns with your soul's path, you create space for the new ones that do. Bless and release those relationships it's time to let go with loving compassion and an appreciation for the purpose they have served in your life.

I lovingly release any relationship that no longer aligns with my soul's path.

BLESS AND RELEASE

*"To attract loving and connected relationships, we must
first embody the love and connection we seek."*

– DR. DEBRA REBLE

A powerful tool to let go of negative energy and clear your body,
mind, and spirit is the mantra, "Bless and release." Every time
you notice a negative thought, feeling, or pattern, think or say,
"Bless and release" to clear any negative energy.

When any person or situation triggers a negative emotion, bless
them (or it) for bringing this unhealed part of yourself into your
awareness. Follow this mantra with opening your heart and sitting
with these emotions. Then release whatever pain surfaces, so it
doesn't become an energy block.

I bless and release any negative
energy in my body, mind, and spirit.

TRUSTING THE PROCESS

"To fuel and feed the soul, remember to unplug to plug in."

– LORE RAYMOND

Sometimes you may feel frustrated, disheartened, or even at a standstill on your spiritual journey. You want to hurry up and get to your destination without any more spiritual detours or backtracking. However, just when you think you have done all spiritual work necessary, you will find more subtle layers of patterns to release and deeper pockets of pain to heal.

You must realize that spiritual transformation requires a commitment for your lifetime. It's not a goal that can be attained, but rather a spiritual progression. Transformation ebbs and flows with periods of intense forward movement which gives way to transitional pauses. An intense growth spurt often requires a rest period to integrate the new energies and experiences that have awakened fully.

I have already chosen the next step forward on my spiritual path even when it feels like I'm standing still.

PRECIOUS SELF-CARE

"When love is flowing through us, we are powerful to co-create whatever our heart desires."

– DR. DEBRA REBLE

Taking precious care of you supports a loving and cherished relationship with yourself. When you take precious care of yourself, you nurture yourself with the utmost love and attention, just as you would someone you cherish.

Engaging in precious self-care may require that you say "no" to others so you can say "yes" to yourself. Often the pattern of obligation can trigger feelings such as "I must" or "I should" be doing for someone else instead of putting yourself first. Be aware of your vulnerability to this pattern and support yourself by saying, "I am taking precious care of myself so that I'm better able to care for others."

Through engaging in self-care, you have more positive energy to give and share with others. It's a win-win for everybody.

I take precious care of myself just
as I would someone I love.

YOUR SPIRITUAL GPS

"Follow your Divine team's nudge and take the leap of faith to fulfill your soul's purpose. You'll create miracles for yourself and others."

– CORNELIA WARD

Like a spiritual GPS, conscious awareness is your intuitive ability to tune in to information which provides you with a broader perspective from which to navigate your life. It bypasses logical thinking and leads to an inner knowing through your heart.

Using conscious awareness, you can access a greater wealth of information to support your spiritual growth. In doing so, you can see with the eyes of your heart and this shifts you from viewing life in only physical terms to seeing why things happen from an expanded, more spiritual, perspective.

I open my heart and listen to the voice of my spirit guiding me.

SURRENDER CONTROL

*"It is only through sharing our shadows that we walk in the light.
Real unshakable joy sources from within, from our light."*

– DR. DEBRA REBLE

When you let go of your need to control, you tap into an unlimited source of positive energy and creativity. If you notice that you are trying to micromanage everyone and everything, you are feeling out of control within yourself. The need to control usually surfaces when you feel fear or anxiety.

You cannot control the feelings or actions of others. Let go, trust yourself, and surrender to the experience and what it is showing you. See it from a spiritual perspective and trust that it is giving you new information about yourself.

I let go of my need to control
and trust that everything will
fall into place.

CREATE A SAFE HAVEN

*"In each moment, make the best decision you can.
Reflect on your life and see how each one brought you
to this special place with no regret."*

– DEBBIE SAIN-BISSETTE

Cultivating healthy intimate relationships requires eliminating emotional baggage. You may have entered into a relationship with baggage that feels like a heavy trunk rather than a carry-on bag. This trunk may be filled with suppressed emotions you have carried and never released because you haven't felt safe enough to do so.

Create a safe haven of love where you feel free to express and let go of your fears and insecurities. Such sacred space supports you to venture into deeper intimacy with another person and feel acknowledged for who you are. Feeling secure within yourself and putting your heart "out there" supports others to step into real intimacy with you.

I create a safe space to freely
express myself without judgment
or censorship.

TRANSFORMING LOSSES

*"Intentional creativity time allows me to align
with my soul, nurture my faith, breath in my purpose,
and intuitively inspire others."*

– DEB "GYPSYOWL" BRYAN

Transforming your losses into love allows you to let go of the past, better appreciate the present, and harness this energy to co-create a more positive future. It opens you to embrace these natural life cycles as a series of births and deaths that ultimately lead to your spiritual progression.

Embracing your losses helps you to face and experience the other side of grief, which is unconditional self-love and self-trust. The strength of love energy empowers you to let go, lean into your pain, and create a transformational shift in your life.

I embrace my losses and
transform them into love.

FOLLOW YOUR INTUITION

"Through my feminine spirit, I make love with life,
play with passion, and live on purpose in every moment."

– DR. DEBRA REBLE

When you follow your intuition, you realize this leads to a richer, more expansive way to live—even when your intuition takes you down a more challenging path. It's essential to act on your intuitive hunches without overthinking, as intuition comes from your heart and spirit.

Trust your inner wisdom and let it assist you with daily problems. You will find you waste less valuable time and energy being anxious about life's difficulties. If something doesn't feel aligned with your true self, trust your intuition and change the situation as soon as possible. Doing so allows you to respond rather than react to life's events, giving you even greater peace of mind.

I pay attention to my intuition
and trust this inner wisdom
without reservation.

LEAD WITH YOUR HEART

*"We all have a divine inheritance encoded
in our sacred hearts. When we discover that pearl of
great price, we never doubt our worth again!"*

– MARCIA MARINER

Observe how you speak to yourself and if your voice is coming from your head or your heart. You can learn to differentiate between the voices of your head (negative/fear-based) and your heart (positive/trust-based) by merely noticing the words you use to describe your everyday experience.

Your heart's voice is loving, kind, and guides you without judgment. It whispers, "I know, I trust, and I sense." The voice of your head, on the other hand, is often critical and judgmental. It says, "I should, I think, and I believe."

Tune in to your heart's voice by observing the dialogue between your head and heart, always choosing to follow your heart.

I lead with my heart and
then use my head.

HEALTHY DETACHMENT

"Define success on your own terms, achieve it by your own rules, and build a life you're proud to live."

– ANNE SWEENEY

Practice healthy detachment by letting go of any expected result. Having expectations of yourself or others can set you up for stress or disappointment. Attachments to specific results can prevent the possibility of even better outcomes happening by keeping you locked within your limited expectations.

Although your expectations may be positive, you still impede the flow of energy by focusing on a specific outcome. Instead, trust you will receive exactly what you need for your transformation at a particular time.

I let go of my expectations
and remain detached from any
specific result.

BE THE BLESSING

*"The empowered voice is the voice of the heart speaking its
truth with intelligence, compassion, and courage."*

– KATHLEEN GUBITOSI, MA

Whether you travel abroad or down the street, move through
your life as a love ambassador. Make your home, workplace,
town, or country better through your caring choices and
positive energies. Emit light and love wherever you go, and with
whomever you meet.

You have an opportunity in every moment not only to bless the
space you occupy but to also "be the blessing," by being
a positive, emanating, and clear presence of light.

I travel through life as
a love ambassador.

HEALING OLD WOUNDS

"As you become more clear about who you really are, you'll be better able to decide what is best for you - the first time around."

– OPRAH

Sometimes a crisis such as a serious illness, trauma, or loss forces you to open to intense transformation. In some ways, change—even the hard change of healing old wounds—is easier when the alternative is unthinkable. Yet, only when you lean into and release the emotional pain can you bring about self-healing.

Until you allow yourself time alone to release your pain, you may not even realize that your body holds on to it. To heal yourself, you have to expose these wounds to the light and reveal all the ways you've been striving to protect them and keep them hidden.

I create a safe space to heal
my past wounds.

TRUST WHATEVER COMES

"To attract abundance, we have to let go of being in control and trust that while like inevitably attracts like, it does so in keeping with its own divine timing."

– DR. DEBRA REBLE

Life presents you with the opportunity to flow gracefully through challenges every day. In such moments when faced with an unexpected situation, you can feel anxious, unprepared, or a sense of futility. When this happens, you are called to let go, lean into trust, and "go with the flow."

By trusting yourself and your connection with a divine source, you remain open to this positive flow of energy. Accept any situation, no matter how painful or difficult, as an opportunity for your transformation.

I trust that whatever comes into my life is what I need for my transformation.

SPEAK FROM THE HEART

"Often change happens in increments over time.
Sometimes it rips you apart to create something new on the spot.
Both ways work."

– NETTIE OWENS

Speak your truth from your heart and accept your experience
as valid and worthwhile even though it may differ from another
person's point of view. Be courageous, lead with your heart,
and reveal your truth—your innermost thoughts, feelings, and
experiences—openly and honestly. Dare to express who
you are fully.

Surround yourself with people who listen openly, respond
meaningfully, and support your need to be heard and
acknowledged for who you are.

I fully express my truth and know
that it is valid and worthwhile.

SHIFT YOUR GAZE

"Commit to discovering, acknowledging, appreciating, owning, and honoring your personal gifts."

– SARAH BAN BREATHNACH

Like a periscope, you can lift your gaze out of the shadowy aspects of human consciousness and obtain a more elevated, spiritual perspective. You are, first and foremost, a spiritual being navigating the sea of human processes. You have the power to open your heart, raise your vibration, and dissolve negativity.

When you act from this elevated perspective, you move beyond the polarized patterns of good/bad, win/lose, and right/wrong. You allow others their viewpoints and genuinely love them even when you disagree or hold a different perspective. Your goal is not to oppose those who hold these polarized patterns, but rather to support those who have committed their lives to a higher vibration of love.

I am in love and at peace with myself, my fellow beings, and the world.

BALANCE YOUR ENERGIES

"Loving ourselves enough to reveal our deepest vulnerabilities is the most courageous choice we can make."

– DR. DEBRA REBLE

Creating balance in your life is a key to enhancing your health, relationships, and well-being. You may be experiencing a particularly intense period of healing, self-discovery, and transformation. Find your inner balance by trusting yourself and moving through these challenging times with lightness, love, and an inner knowing of what's core to your soul.

Balance your energies by taking precious care of yourself and letting go of more in your life than ever before. Prioritize the things you hold dear to you: the relationships, experiences, and soul elements of your life. Strive for balance by investing more of your time and energies in what aligns with your soul's journey.

I create balance in my life by focusing on what is core to my soul.

IN THE FLOW

"Listening to your heart is not simple. Finding out who you are is not simple. It takes a lot of hard work and courage to get to know who you are and what you want."

– SUE BENDER

Sustaining a positive flow of energy is the key to manifesting a happy, fulfilling, and peaceful life. It is more than the power of positive thinking that creates a state of happiness; it is the flow of energy that you channel positively and productively.

The unending flow of positive energy that you exude affects every aspect of your life—how you wake up in the morning, carry yourself, handle disappointment, and give and receive love. Using energy in this way, you make impeccable choices that bring you the love, joy, and well-being you desire.

I sustain a positive flow of energy which brings me love, joy, and well-being.

BEGIN WITH GRATITUDE

*"Isn't it beautiful that we have the opportunity to change
the lives of others by simply making our self-care
a visible practice from time to time?"*

– JESSICA DUGAS

Begin your day in gratitude, knowing there are challenges ahead.
Trust that you are never given more than you can handle. Put your
hand on your heart and list five things for which you're grateful.
This energy of love opens your heart, expands your awareness,
and sets a positive tone for your day.

Appreciate what shows up in your life and be flexible with how
the day unfolds instead of forcing your expectations upon it.
Gently remind yourself that "this too shall pass" when you
stay constant in the flow of positive energy no matter what is
unfolding before you.

I am grateful for and prepared
to handle any challenge that
presents itself today.

LIVE ON PURPOSE

"You may have a fresh start any moment you choose,
for this thing that we call 'failure' is not the falling down,
but the staying down."

– MARY PICKFORD

You have a soul purpose, not a sole purpose, to live every moment expressing the light of your being. Your soul's purpose isn't defined or limited by finding the one reason you are here; it encompasses a multitude of passions that inspire soul-hearted living as a meditation through life.

Be love, make your dreams a reality, and assist others to do the same. Stay aligned with your soul's path and co-create the life you envision. Live purposefully in every moment no matter what you are doing, where you are, or whom you are with.

I live on purpose through
expressing the light of my being.

LIVE FULLY EXPRESSED

"When, as a parent, you live as an ambassador of love yourself, you inspire your child to express positive energy and a healthy optimism for their future and the future of the world."

– DR. DEBRA REBLE

Taking charge of your destiny requires you to nurture a more conscious relationship with yourself and become accountable for your life. Be aware of every thought, feeling, and choice you make, especially the flow of energy you bring to every moment.

The intrinsic power to realize your dreams begins with trusting yourself and choosing to live fully expressed, no matter what is happening in your life. It's up to you to fulfill your soul's potential and attract, develop, and sustain the most inspiring and fulfilling relationships possible to support it.

I am accountable for the flow of energy I bring to every moment.

VIBRATION OF LOVING WORDS

*"Following your inner light and living your truth allows
you to draw your future into the present and to fully
start loving your life now."*

– LAURA P. CLARK

Engaging in open, honest, and compassionate communication promotes a deepening of trust and intimacy with yourself and in your relationships. It connects your heart and soul with others.

The vibration of loving words has a positive effect where negative words can damage and destroy. When you speak from your heart, love energy permeates your words and infuses your tone of voice. It opens a safe and sacred space for others to hear you—all the more reason to practice speaking your truth from your heart.

All I think, speak, and do brings
beauty, harmony, and love into
the world.

HONOR YOUR NEEDS

*"Take time each day to connect with the earth beneath you.
Breathe in the fresh air, and feel the earth beneath your feet."*

– FELICIA D'HAITI

Creating healthy energetic boundaries produces a positive flow
of energy in your relationships. With such boundaries in place,
the flow of energy is growth-promoting, first for yourself and
then for others. Without these boundaries, you can easily exhaust
yourself or take on the unwanted energies of others.

Honor your need for personal time and engage in activities that
restore and revitalize your energies. Doing this will give you more
vitality and stamina to serve others. Making this commitment to
yourself benefits everyone in your world. So breathe, let go, and
let it all be.

I support a loving relationship with
myself and others by creating healthy
energetic boundaries.

REVEAL YOUR TRUE SELF

"Something which we think is impossible now is not impossible in another decade."

– CONSTANCE BAKER MOTLEY

Sharing your innermost thoughts and feelings with another allows you to forge an intimate and meaningful relationship. When you reveal your true being to someone else, you can bridge any chasm that separates with such intimacy. Revealing yourself can be uncomfortable at first, but it is emotionally fulfilling to relate to others in such a deep and real way.

Revealing your true self can bring you closer together, and your intimate connection gives you a common ground upon which to grow in relationship spiritually. Open your heart and be brave enough to reveal yourself. Then, reciprocate and truly see the other person, too.

I reveal my true self to create
an intimate and soul-connected
relationship.

FOLLOW YOUR HEART

"Making a compassionate covenant with yourself to practice at least one act of self-care act every day can sustain calm when you find yourself in the midst of chaos."

– DR. DEBRA REBLE

When you follow your heart, you live with passion and purpose. You feel a sense of alignment with your soul's journey. You realize your full self-expression is higher than the job you perform, the roles you play, or how successful you are in the world.

Follow your heart no matter what anyone else thinks. Let go of anything in your life that no longer serves you and choose what is more appropriate to your real being at this moment in time.

I choose to follow my heart and live with passion and purpose.

UNCONDITIONAL SELF-LOVE

"Find the gift in everything that happens. Sometimes your greatest gifts show up in the ugliest wrapping."

– KELLY MISHELL

Self-love leads to acceptance of the spiritual nature of your true self. Deeper than your identity or roles you play is your true being—your sense of oneness, aliveness, and authentic relatedness. You can experience self-love by opening your heart and allowing pure love to flow through you.

Unconditionally loving yourself is the foundation for developing soul-hearted relationships. Through soul connections with others, you can see that you are no longer separate, but rather one in the collective flow of genuine love.

Loving myself connects my heart
and soul with others.

CO-CREATING WITH SOURCE

"One of the most courageous things you can do is identify yourself, know who you are, what you believe in and where you want to go."

– SHEILA MURRAY BETHEL

Just as a plane is guided into the air, you, as a co-pilot with source, are guiding your intentions into reality. With absolute trust that one moment will unfold perfectly into the next, let go of any expectations, specific outcomes, or preconceived plans.

Take a deep breath and release any fear of your life not going as you planned. Trust that you are co-creating the exact life experience you need and it's unfolding right in front of you. Stay open to the positive flow of energy that leads you through any challenge and co-creates an outcome beyond what you ever thought possible.

I trust that I am co-creating with my source the experiences I need.

TRANSFORMING PAIN

"If you have knowledge, let others light their candles in it."

– MARGARET FULLER

Despite the deep pain it elicits, loss teaches us about the delicate balance, intensity, and richness of life. You cannot experience the pain of loss without first having experienced the joys associated with what has been lost.

Your heartbreak also connects you to the collective loss that everyone has experienced in their lives and reveals any wounds you haven't healed. It gives you the opportunity to release your unresolved pain. Like stripping away layers of paint to reveal handcrafted woodwork, you can peel away the layers of pain through transforming them into something exquisite…into love.

I release my layers of pain and transform them into love.

CHOOSING HAPPINESS

*"To give love more generously, we have
to receive love more graciously."*

– DR. DEBRA REBLE

Choose to be happy. Happiness is the purest state of being-well-being. Yet, you may feel that happiness lies outside of your reach, that it's elusive or unattainable. Happiness is within your grasp, and you have the power to create it in your life.

Sustaining a flow of happiness requires incorporating these spiritual practices into your everyday life: flexibility, self-love, a positive outlook, gratitude, mindfulness, savoring, kindness, being in nature, forgiveness, and playfulness. Let go of any old habits that have inhibited your happiness and make these practices your new healthy ones.

I choose to be happy today
and every day.

YOUR SOUL'S PATH

*"Being open to receiving guidance from the universe is like
putting a neon sign out on your energy field saying,
"positive assistance is welcome here."*

– KRIS GROTH

Nurture a kind, patient, and loving, relationship with yourself,
and you set the groundwork for a lifelong journey of spiritual
transformation. Trust yourself and your connection to source,
listen to the voice of your heart, and make intentions for a more
fulfilling life. Let go of the life you have chosen until now so you
can co-create the life you want in your future.

Witness how spirit guides you to opportunities and choices which
result in a life based on spiritual transformation. Once you have
transformed any aspect of yourself, you move forward on your
soul's path.

I let go of the life I have to
co-create the life I want.

PATHWAY TO PEACE

"Do you want to meet the love of your life? Look in the mirror."
– BYRON KATIE

Compassion is the pathway to inner peace and happiness.
It infuses love into every encounter with both you and others.
When you live as a compassionate being, you trust that every
human being is on their own spiritual path. This awareness
increases your capacity to create peace and harmony in your life
because it shows you the interconnectedness of all beings and
that you are a part of the universal energy of love.

Widening your circle of compassion and practicing non-violence
begins with you. It starts with halting the harsh, critical thoughts,
words, and actions you inflict upon yourself, then onto others.

All that I am, do, and express
returns to me as love.

FEARLESS LIVING

*"A woman is the full circle. Within her is the power
to create, nurture and transform."*

– DIANE MARIECHILD

Fearless living takes more than deep breaths and positive
mantras; it takes absolute trust in yourself and the courage of
the heart. Letting go of fear and trusting yourself goes hand in
hand, as one supports the other. The more you let go, the more
you learn to trust yourself; the more you trust yourself, the
more you can let go.

Letting go of fear is a doorway to freedom and co-creating
the life you've always dreamed of. Instead of staying stuck in
fear, courageously take those wobbly steps and move forward
toward your desires. Make the conscious choice to shift from
fear into trust.

I trust that everything always works
out for my highest good.

EMBRACING HOPE

"Creating balance in our lives is key to enhancing our health, relationships, and wellbeing."

– DR. DEBRA REBLE

View your life through the eyes of your heart with love, optimism, and hope. Awaken to this new perspective by planting seeds of love to open and flourish in your heart. Reflect positive possibilities and mirror to others the love you see. When you transfuse someone with love and hope, you empower them.

Hope makes it possible not only to endure hardship but to make the best of any challenging situation. It brings you peace in the midst of turmoil. Let spirit lift you out of your earthly woes and into a trust that all is well. Keeping your dreams alive, keeps hope alive in your heart.

When I keep my dreams alive,
I keep hope alive in my heart.

COURAGE OF HEART

"Creating balance in our lives is key to enhancing our health, relationships, and wellbeing."

– FELICIA D'HAITI

Embracing your vulnerabilities is the most courageous choice you can make. Courage is the intrinsic power you have to confront your hurts, fears, and imperfections. When you face your vulnerable pain, you will uncover who you truly are and the power in the universe that is your birthright.

Lean into the uncomfortableness so you can feel your vulnerable pain. In this safe and sacred space, let fear and resistance step aside and allow your insecurities to surface and release. Experiencing your vulnerability is the catalyst for your physical, emotional, and spiritual healing.

I face my vulnerabilities
with courage of heart.

LET IT BE

"Setting boundaries are critical to nurturing ourselves as it reinforces the importance of listening to our feelings and acknowledging what we need."

– KELLEY GRIMES, MSW

Simply saying to yourself, "Let it be," tells your brain that you have entered a no judgment zone. In this space, release your attachment to a person or situation and eliminate any negativity or resistance. "Letting it be" encourages compassion, forgiveness, and acceptance of your own and others' spiritual paths.

Follow your heart and move through each day without trying to control others or events. When you give way to the need to control, you give away your self-control. Soften your positions, trust yourself to create positive intentions, and make discerning choices.

I let things be and lead
with my heart.

WHOLEHEARTED LOVE

"Every time you don't follow your inner guidance,
you feel a loss of energy, loss of power,
a sense of spiritual deadness."

– SHAKTI GAWAIN

To fall in love is magical; to flow in love is mystical. When you fall in love, you get a glimpse of your lover's soul. When you flow in love, all impediments fall away, and your lover's soul is all you see. By flowing in love with someone, you engage in the ultimate dance of soul-hearted partnership, sharing your joy, passion, and exuberance for life.

Flowing in love takes a harmonious balance of giving and receiving love without expectation. You become an energetic conduit for directing this flow of love to co-create your reality. When directed with intention, this energy source becomes the catalyst to co-creating soul-hearted relationships in your life.

I express love wholeheartedly
and without reservation.

YOU ARE LOVE

"By blessing whatever space we occupy with our divine presence, we become an emanating field of love to others and our world."

– DR. DEBRA REBLE

You dream of love, you yearn for love, and you make love, but rarely do you realize that you are love. You may view love as something to attain, to have, and to hold. You may even think you have to prove yourself worthy of love.

Yet, love isn't something you strive for, but rather a flow of divine energy that you are. When you know beyond any doubt that you are loveable, love becomes the source from which all of your thoughts, words, and choices flow.

I am whole and complete love.

FREEDOM IN FORGIVENESS

"Remember that loving yourself and nourishing your spirit is loving the family you care for, and there is no better way to start your day than connecting with the beauty inside you."

– KRISTINE CARLSON

The greatest gift you can give yourself—at this moment—is forgiveness, for it sets you free. It transforms judgment into acceptance and makes the past powerless over you. Find the courage to forgive yourself and others, the strength to suspend judgment, and the compassion to release your pain.

Forgiveness allows you to create a clean slate so you can begin anew. The more you forgive yourself, the easier you'll find it to forgive others. You'll be freed from the past and open energetic space for you to create a better future.

I am open and willing to forgive
myself and others.

COURAGEOUS AUTHENTICITY

"If you don't have a clear signal to your intuition, then both your incoming & outgoing communication will be unclear."

– CRYSTAL COCKERHAM

It takes real courage to express who you are in the world. Courage, which comes from the Latin word for "heart," sources deep within your heart as self-acceptance and compassion. It encourages you to embrace every situation, no matter how scary, as an opportunity for spiritual transformation.

To be courageous is to lead with your heart, and speak your truth, honestly and openly. It's daring to express who you are without reservation fully. You don't think or feel your way into being courageous; you take inspired action.

I courageously express who I am
without reservation.

MORE THAN ENOUGH

"Love resonates, at our heart center, our minds, infinitely. It grows abundantly in a purposeful life of joy, gratitude, and peace."

– BONNIE LARSON

Creating a flow of abundance in your life takes a harmonious balance of giving and receiving. To give more generously, you have to receive more graciously. This mutual exchange of energy creates an abundance of all that is good.

Your life will be filled with prosperity when you trust that there is more than enough to go around. Acknowledging the blessings you already have in your life shifts your mindset from scarcity to abundance. Align your intentions for the greater good of all, and you will generate more abundance in all areas of your life.

I give generously and receive graciously which leads to abundance.

TRUSTING YOURSELF

"When you activate and trust your superpower
of intuition, your life magically becomes clear, authentic,
purposeful, joyful and easy!"

– CAROLYN MCGEE

Trust yourself and let go so you can see your vulnerabilities in a new light. Instead of avoiding your fears, hurts, and imperfections, courageously embrace them to create an authentic and loving relationship with yourself.

To trust yourself is to love yourself even when you feel unlovable, to make loving choices for yourself even when you feel unworthy, and to open yourself to love even when you're afraid of being hurt. Trusting yourself allows you to participate fully in life without holding back any part of yourself.

I embrace my vulnerability as a
pathway to uncovering my true self.

FOCUS ON THE FLOW

*"Keeping an open heart sustains unconditional love
in a conditional world."*

– DR. DEBRA REBLE

Come home to your heart, the seat of your soul, inner wisdom, and spiritual truth. Begin by closing your eyes, and, placing a hand on the center of your chest, focus your attention on your heart. Breathe in love, gratitude, and compassion. Breathe out anxiety, negativity, and tension.

Focus on the flow of energy emanating from your heart and feel your body, mind, and spirit move into vibrational harmony. Allow your brain and nervous system to calm down and align with the ebb and flow of your heart rhythms.

By opening my heart, I bring my
body, mind, and spirit into harmony.

YOU ARE THE SOURCE

"I think the key is for women not to set any limits."

– MARTINA NAVRATILOVA

Love is your birthright. You were born as pure love—an infinite, all-encompassing energy source without limits or conditions. Acknowledge that you are divine energy and see the essence of yourself as love.

You are the source, the origin of this pure energy that flows through you, which is also referred to as light, God, higher power, universal energy, or divine intelligence. The energy of God is the acknowledgment of love within yourself and others.

I am the divine source of love.

RELEASE THE PAST

"What we do for a living is not the truth of who we are.
It is who we are at a soul level in our quietest moments
of being that truly matters."

– LINDA JOY

To clear your fear and progress spiritually, you must release all that you hold on to from your past. Everything from your past, especially your thoughts, can create energy blocks that interfere with the full expression of who you are. The present moment is all there is; celebrate your past, and release it.

Let go of the positive as well as the negative, the things from which you draw strength as well as those that drag you down. When you are no longer holding on to anything, you can fully trust spirit to guide your life. You will experience a rebirth into an even more magnificent expression.

I let go of the past, celebrate
the present, and trust spirit to
guide my future.

CONNECT TO SOURCE

*"The most common way people give up their power
is by thinking they don't have any."*

– ALICE WALKER

Acknowledge yourself as a strong, sensitive, and intuitive being,
connected to your divine source. Become aware of your thoughts,
feelings, and intuitions. Pay attention to the moments of clarity
which occur unexpectedly. Be open to the spiritual guidance
coming through your heart, and act on it without reservation.

Listening to your intuition is listening to spirit, an invisible best
friend. Open to the spiritual information you receive, trust its
source, and use it to guide your life.

I am a strong, sensitive,
and intuitive person connected
to my divine source.

MIRACLE OF LOVE

"Life shrinks or expands in proportion to one's courage."

– ANAIS NIN

Where love is present, there are always miracles. Miracles occur when you expand your awareness and sustain a flow of positive energy, no matter what is happening in your life.

Trust that there is more to your life than what you experience on a physical level. The universe co-creates with you, not against you. Miracles are divine opportunities for the universe to show you it's got your back. Miracles are present in your life and always show up when you need them, with divine timing.

I am the miracle of love.

DIVINE SYNCHRONICITY

"One of the lessons that I grew up with was to always stay true to yourself and never let what somebody else says distract you from your goals."

– MICHELLE OBAMA

Trust divine timing rather than human timing and things will flow more smoothly than you could ever imagine. Divine timing, or synchronicity, occurs when you declare your intentions, let go of control and impatience, and allow the universe to co-create with you according to an elevated timetable.

Such synchronistic experiences become more common when you act on intuitions that seem to come out of the blue with no agenda. There's a spiritual timing of events in your life, even when they feel like random coincidences. The occurrence of these coincidental events shows you that the universe is conspiring with you.

I trust that everything unfolds
in divine timing.

BE STILL

*"When you start seeing the truth of your worth, it will
start becoming easier to remove the toxins in your life
that do not serve you."*

– CINDY HIVELY

Create a safe space where you can have a sacred chat with your
inner child. Surround yourself with your favorite scents and
sounds, then curl up in a cozy chair with your journal. Close
your eyes, drop into your heart space, and visualize yourself
as a young child.

Open and allow your heart to soften to the wisdom she holds for
you. Begin your sacred chat by asking her the following questions:
"What wounds do you need me to heal? How do you want to
be loved? What do you need to feel safe?" Be still and allow the
answers to come through your heart and then write them down
in your journal.

I surround my inner child with
pure love from my heart.

ACKNOWLEDGE THE BLESSINGS

"Always concentrate on how far you have come, rather than how far you have left to go. The difference in how easy it seems will amaze you."

– HEIDI JOHNSON

Acknowledge the blessings of who you are and what you already have. Over the course of the day, keep a journal of the things for which you're grateful. Share the good things that happen today with a friend or partner. Go out of your way to show gratitude when others assist you.

As your day begins, repeat the mantra, "I am a blessed being." Bring to mind three things that you feel grateful for or happy about, even if it's just being alive. When your day comes to a close, reflect on three things that happened during the day that you feel blessed about, and how you believe they happened for you.

I am grateful for all the blessings in my life.

INFINITE SOURCE OF LOVE

"The thing that is really hard, and really amazing, is giving up on being perfect and beginning the work of becoming yourself."

– ANNA QUINDLEN

You are connected to a field of divine energy that emanates from you. Consciously plug into this energy source through prayer, meditation, being in nature, or mindfulness. Connect with your infinite source of love and live every day as a sacred meditation.

Sit quietly, place your hand on your heart, and visualize a pearl of white light in the center of your chest. Allow this light to expand outward as a radiant beam of light connecting you with the power of the universe. Feel the energy flow as it comes back to you through your heart.

I open my heart and connect to the infinite energy of the universe.

YOUR SOUL SUPPORT TEAM

"Everyone has inside of her a piece of good news. The good news is that you don't know how great you can be! How much you can love! What you can accomplish! And what your potential is!"

– ANNE FRANK

The only thing that really matters is spending time with those you love. Surround yourself with people who love, support, and care for you without conditions. Create an energetic soul support team consisting of people who encourage you without judging, enabling, or commiserating.

Share your truth with those who not only have your backs but, most of all, your heart. Such soul support comes from kindred spirits who encourage the full expression of your being rather than your identity or roles you play to survive in the world. They motivate you to trust yourself and follow your heart.

I create an energetic soul support team who loves me unconditionally.

SPIRITUAL FEEDBACK

"The journey to healing and inner peace isn't about being strong; it's about taking off your mask and being vulnerable."

– MICHELE GREER

Trust that your spirit is stronger than any challenge you can possibly face. Accept every situation as an opportunity for transformation, even when the situation unravels the fabric of your life. Focus on the light in the darkness, and affirm your strength in handling whatever comes your way.

Trust that you can transform your life by accepting what's right in front of you, even when it's painful or challenging. Welcome this spiritual feedback from the universe and incorporate this information into your life.

I trust I can handle anything
that comes my way.

MIRACLE OF CREATION

*"Breaking out of our comfort zones challenges
us to expand our range of spiritual understanding
and stimulate our personal growth."*

– DR. DEBRA REBLE

You are a miracle of creation. You have this divine power within you. Unleash this force of light and love energy on any physical or emotional issue you need to heal. Source this energy through your heart and surround every cell in your body with it for healing. Like light streams, direct this energy with the highest intention to heal any dis-ease in your body.

Raise your energies to the vibration of love where miracles occur. Raising your vibration initiates an energetic shift which catalyzes all the physical resources you need for healing.

I channel light energy to heal
my mind and body.

A CHILDLIKE SPIRIT

*"Be courageous step into your life fully with your
heart wide open. The Universe is waiting for you
to say 'yes' to yourself."*

– ANNA-CHARLOTTE HANDLER

Spend time playing, having fun, and celebrating your true being.
Enjoy your sensuous nature and take pleasure in the simple
things, which bring you joy. Say yes to new situations, which make
you laugh, explore outside your comfort zone, and prompt a
new perspective. Bring a sense of humor and silliness into every
moment, and refuse to take life seriously.

Open to your childlike spirit every day by creating experiences
that infuse into your everyday life awe, wonder, and delight.

I open to my childlike spirit and
play with joyful abandon.

EASE AND GRACE

"Your own words are the bricks and mortar of the dreams you want to realize. Your words are the greatest power you have. The words you choose and their use establish the life you experience."

– SONIA CHOQUETTE

When you live in the flow of love, you trust the divine order that exists in everything around and within you. Surrender any expectations of how your life should be, and focus your intentions on how you want it to be.

Align yourself with this natural flow, release your perceived control, and move effortlessly through your daily experiences. As a result, your feelings of anxiety ease and you fully engage in each moment with a deeper level of awe, wonder, and enjoyment. Live in the flow of love and create a simpler, more authentic way of living.

I live in the flow of love which creates a life of ease and grace.

QUIET REFLECTION

*"Committing to nurturing ourselves opens us
to the infinite possibilities of self-awareness, self-compassion,
mindfulness, gratitude, and self-love."*

– KELLEY GRIMES, MSW

Spend time alone in quiet reflection, whether meditating, sitting
in a garden, looking out a window, or writing in a journal. Begin
with five minutes at the beginning and end of each day, then
gradually increase the time. Create a sacred space for going
within and becoming self-aware. Observe and reflect on your
vulnerable feelings.

Be compassionate company with yourself, as if spending time
with an old, trusted friend whom you unconditionally love and
accept. Lean into your tender places and discover that your loving
friend has been there all along.

I spend time alone to reflect and
become more self-aware.

LIGHTHEARTED SPIRIT

*"I don't want to get to the end of my life and find that
I lived just the length of it. I want to have lived
the width of it as well."*

– DIANE ACKERMAN

Having a sense of humor cultivates lightheartedness. It connects you to the depths of your soul and is crucial in healing your body. When you laugh with others, you share a sense of interconnectedness which assists in healing as well.

Soul laughter originates deep within and assists you in intimately communing with others. When you share your vulnerabilities, you communicate a loving presence heart to heart without spoken words. Such soul giggles strengthen your connection with others and give you a more buoyant outlook on life.

I am lighthearted when I laugh
from the depths of my soul.

A PEACEFUL SHIFT

"Embracing change is a creative process that opens us up to new possibilities. Imagine living your life from that perspective."

– PAMELA THOMPSON

Open your heart and be in present awareness. This is where acceptance, compassion, and trust of yourself and a divine source live. Fear cannot coexist in the same space as trust.

Drop into your heart space and feel centered and grounded even as anxious thoughts spiral through your mind. Bring your attention from your head to your heart and create a peaceful shift in your energies. This calms your anxiety-ridden brain and nervous system; it also brings your body and mind into energetic balance with your heart energy.

When I drop into my heart center,
I create a peaceful shift in
my energies.

INVITE IN BLESSINGS

"A woman is like a tea bag —you never know how strong she is until she gets in hot water."

– ELEANOR ROOSEVELT

Invite in blessings of love, peace, and abundance and let go of any fear and negativity. Complete every moment with gratitude, compassion, and forgiveness for everyone and everything that has brought you to this point in your life.

Stay centered, love yourself, and clear your life of anything that is no longer aligned with your true being. Give yourself the freedom to follow your heart and make the impeccable choices to support your soul's path. Be a force of light, love, and all that is good.

I invite in blessings of love
and let go of fear.

EMBRACE THE MESSINESS

"We are so used to giving more power to visible outside circumstances than to the power of our invisible intention wedded with faith that we often simply don't allow the gifts of the universe into our lives."

– SUSYN REEVE

Awakening to your authentic self leads you to let go of who you think you should be and embrace who you are. Living authentically is like singing karaoke. At first, you may be nervous; yet each time you trust yourself and surrender your need for perfection, you live "out loud."

Don't be afraid to make a mistake, make a mess, or displease someone. Embrace these messy, imperfect parts of yourself. Override your negative beliefs about yourself, release what other people think, and express yourself, heart and soul.

I release the need to be perfect and all that inhibits my full self-expression.

SPEAK WITH LOVE

*"To give love more generously, you have
to receive love more graciously."*

– DR. DEBRA REBLE

Live authentically by courageously communicating from your heart.
Speak your truth—your intimate thoughts and feelings—honestly
and openly, without holding back. Allow your words to come from
your heart, and they will have a more profound meaning to the
listener. Sincere, honest, and loving words encourage others to
listen to you; they are like nectar that draws thirsty bees to a flower.

I speak my truth from an
open and loving heart.

FROM PANIC TO PEACE

"Comparing yourself with another does nothing more than overshadow your own brilliance, beauty, and uniqueness. You have qualities and attributes that no other has so why them hide behind comparison?"

– PAM THOMAS

Using empowering affirmations can shift you from panic to peace. They help relieve anxiety, calm the mind and body, and elevate your vibration to a higher level, especially when you feel the lower vibrations from fear, self-doubt, or powerlessness.

Replace any negative thoughts with positive affirmations such as, "I am love, I am safe, and I trust my connection to my source." Repeat these affirmations throughout the day, focus your attention on the positive events in your life, and catch and release your negative thoughts and the anxieties they trigger.

I replace my negative thoughts
with positive affirmations.

GUIDE YOUR INTENTIONS

"We have the power to change our lives by looking at all parts of our truth and then working to heal what no longer serves us."

– DR. CATHERINE HAYES, CPCC

Guide your intentions into reality by co-navigating with your source. Visualize yourself out in front of your intention and imagine how your manifested intention would look and feel in your life. As you go about your day, think and act as if your intention has already manifested.

Be fully open to the spiritual information that comes through your heart. Act on this information and make the inspired choices that bring this intention into reality. When you feel in resonance with the information, you can make an inspired choice. When you feel doubtful, pause making any decision until it feels in divine alignment.

I am co-creating my intentions
with my source and open
to new possibilities.

GUIDANCE OF YOUR HEART

*"Women need real moments of solitude and self-reflection
to balance out how much of ourselves we give away."*

– BARBARA DE ANGELIS

Your purpose for getting out of bed in the morning derives from
connecting with your soul through your heart. Become aware of
the experiences that inspire you, create joy, or make your heart
sing. Notice the soul elements that run through these experiences
and let them guide you to make more inspired choices.

Listen to the guidance of your heart and live purposefully instead of
drifting through life without a compass. This takes ab-soul-lute trust
in yourself and a strong desire to align with your soul's journey.

I listen to the guidance of my
heart and live purposefully.

ALIGN WITH YOUR HEART

*"You are divine energy incarnated in human form.
Healing occurs when you courageously direct your energy
toward your own highest good."*

– KATT TOZIER

Make discerning choices by listening to your heart instead of your head. If something doesn't feel aligned with your true self, trust your intuition, and make a new choice as soon as possible.

Keep following the path you are on as long as things are moving smoothly. When things are not going so well, pause, listen to your heart, and then choose a different path. Let go of the fear of making the wrong choice and trust that you can always choose again and realign with your soul's path.

I make discerning choices by
listening to my heart.

HONOR THE CYCLES

"Where love is present, there are always miracles."

— DR. DEBRA REBLE

Be fully present and notice the beauty in the world around you. Tune into your senses, which turns up the volume on the artistry that surrounds you. Gaze up at the stars, listen to the sounds of a wind chime, or smell the rain. Be mindful of the cycles of the seasons and the moon.

Watch nature unfold in its brilliance and see that it is part of the natural cycles of life and death. Observe how your life parallels the cycles of nature. Embrace these spiritual shifts by letting go, setting new intentions, and conspiring with the energies of the universe.

I am fully present and aware
of the beauty around me.

GRATITUDE OPENS YOUR HEART

*"The joy of knowing yourself, sharing inspiration,
and living your purpose is the most amazing gift. It adds
meaning to everything you do."*

– FELICIA BAUCOM

Begin every day feeling grateful for opportunities to open your heart. No matter what your circumstances, daily bless yourself, your fellow human beings, and the earth; then express appreciation for your unique gifts.

Gratitude opens your heart and helps you hear the voice of your spirit guiding your life. Be thankful for such spiritual guidance. It lets you know that you are not alone on your journey through life and strengthens your connection with the universe.

I open my heart in gratitude for
the day in front of me.

CULTIVATE SELF-COMPASSION

"Enjoy the beauty in the ordinary extraordinary."

– CHARLOTTE BIFULCO

Cultivate self-compassion by being kind and nonjudgmental when you struggle, make a mistake, or feel unworthy. Stop beating yourself up or putting yourself down every time you become aware of an imperfection or expose a vulnerability. Lovingly accept all aspects of yourself without reservation, no matter how you feel about them.

Self-compassion supports your health and well-being. The more lovingly you treat yourself, the more loving you will be toward others. This generates a sense of universal love, inner peace, and spiritual attunement with everyone and everything.

I am kind and nonjudgmental
with myself.

TAKE TIME TO PAUSE

*"Nothing is greater than taking a minute, just
to reflect on God's presence within it."*

– SUSAN KAY DAHL

When faced with a situation that feels uncomfortable, pause, open your heart, and check in with yourself. Notice what is triggering your emotional reaction and then release it before speaking or taking action. Consistently clear any negative energies by blessing and releasing any thoughts, emotions, or energies before they create energy blocks in your body.

Lovingly coach yourself through any challenging situation with supportive self-talk such as, "Open your heart and let go and let it be."

When I feel uncomfortable, I pause,
open my heart, and go within.

TAKE TIME TO PLAY

*"You can do one of two things; just shut up, which is
something I don't find easy, or learn an awful lot very fast,
which is what I tried to do."*

– JANE FONDA

Being playful naturally liberates the mind, opens the heart, and lifts the spirit. It fosters compassion, enhances creativity, and is vital to well-being. In this state of pure being, you feel free to channel this flow of energy beyond any obstacle or limitation.

Remember, when you had thirty minutes for recess? The bell would ring, and for thirty precious minutes, time stood still, and the universe of possibility opened up to you. The bell is ringing, how are you going to play with all the possibilities today?

I allow myself to play and be
open to all the possibilities.

RESTORATIVE SELF-CARE

"Think like a queen. A queen is not afraid to fail.
Failure is another steppingstone to greatness."

– OPRAH

You can practice restorative self-care by performing small acts of kindness toward yourself. Such choices are not self-indulgent, but essential to the well-being of your body, mind, and spirit. Take a few minutes at the beginning and end of every day to meditate, journal, or relax.

Transform your daily shower or bath into a ritual to cleanse your energy field after a stressful day. Engage in activities such as walking, yoga, massage, or energy work to release tension, toxicity, and enhance the flow of positive energy.

I take time to engage in
restorative self-care.

MANIFESTING ABUNDANCE

*"Creating a flow of abundance in our lives
requires a harmonious balance of giving and receiving
without expectations or conditions."*

– DR. DEBRA REBLE

Take time to reflect on what you want to let go of and what you want to bring into your life. Use this as an opportunity to release the situations, people, or patterns in your life that you're ready to release and forgive. Focus on what is appropriate to your being at this time in your life.

Sit quietly, open your heart, and let the flow of energy move through you as you meditate on your intentions. You can write them down and put them in a special place to reflect on at a later time. Trust yourself that you will manifest in your life an abundance of all that is good, loving, and joyful.

I manifest an abundance of all
that is good, loving, and joyful.

SURRENDER THE OUTCOME

*"I'm not the picture of perfection, and for the first time,
I don't want to be. I want to be me: a beautiful,
messy, work in progress."*

– JESSICA DUGAS

Using the power of intention is not about setting a specific goal and focusing on it so much that you lose sight of other possibilities. On the contrary, it is about setting a goal, being open to the many choices that present themselves to reach that goal, then selecting the ones most likely to bring about your desired outcome.

Trust your connection to your source of creation; this ignites your intention, which allows you to see more possibilities, and then take inspired action that will benefit you in the future.

I set my intention, take inspired
action, and then surrender
the outcome.

ONE CHOICE AT A TIME

"Women have an innate capacity of intuition.
Our dreams and our unique energy blueprint want
to be embodied. Give yourself the gift!"

– ANNA-CHARLOTTE HANDLER

Break free of your comfort zones to expand your spiritual perspective and stimulate growth. Even though it may be uncomfortable, uproot the habits and mindsets that keep you stuck in these "deadening zones." Step outside the confines of your comfort zones and move toward what you fear.

Break out of your habits of resistance, avoidance, and control. Embrace change as the constant in your life. Say yes to a new activity, adventure, or creative experience that takes you outside your comfort zone.

I break out of my comfort zones
one choice at a time.

EMBODY LOVE

"Tap into the vibration of gratitude and trust that right now at this moment you have everything you need."

– TARAH ABRAM

Be accountable for the energy that you emit to the world. If your energy is toxic or negative, you will invite toxicity and negativity into your life. If you open your heart and radiate love, you will attract love and connection with others.

When you embody love as your divine essence, you no longer have to search. Like a magnet, love comes to you. You attract soul-connected people into your life by being your own soulmate, responsible for the energy that aligns you with your soul's journey.

I attract soul-connected people into my life by being my own soulmate.

GIVE YOURSELF PERMISSION

"Taking time to be with yourself is at the core of creating and sustaining alignment with your heart, your being, and your soul's journey."

– DR. DEBRA REBLE

You cannot fully release emotional pain with your mind alone, it must be transformed through your heart. By releasing the "heart stuff," you create a sacred space for self-healing where you can be whole again.

Open your heart, lean into your pain, and let go of your unremitting suffering. While uncomfortable in the moment, you can transform the pain into something exquisite: the revelation of who you truly are and how deeply you love. Give yourself permission to rise from the ashes like the phoenix.

I open my heart to my unhealed pain
and transform it into love.

RECOGNIZE YOUR LIGHT

*"In the space between creation and manifestation, it may
appear as if nothing is happening. In these times,
so much is happening. Trust the pause."*

– JOYCE FENNELL

Open your heart and feel the infinite energy of love that connects
you with others. You are not separate but linked together in the
flow of universal love. Like the Hindu gesture of Namaste, open
your heart and recognize the light and love in another. When you
say " I love you" to anyone you are actually saying, "I love myself,
and I give love to you."

I am the source of love and connect
with others through this flow
of energy.

MEMO TO THE UNIVERSE

*"When you surrender, give up the fear thoughts,
and give up the control of a situation, you open the way
for a miracle to take place."*

– IYANLA VANZANT

Every thought, feeling, word, and action you put forth is a memo
to the universe through invisible energetic vibrations. Keep
loving, positive energy in circulation by what you think, feel, say,
and do, and the universe will conspire with you.

You have unlimited creative power to project love out into the
world. Sustain the circulation of loving energy through your
thoughts, words, and choices that benefit yourself and others.

I have unlimited creative power
through my thoughts, words,
and actions.

THE GUIDANCE OF SPIRIT

*"When you forgive, you heal your own anger and hurt
and are able to let love lead again. It's like spring
cleaning for your heart."*

– MARCI SHIMOFF

Focus on the guidance of your heart. Sit in a quiet place and enter a state of present awareness through your breath, prayer, or meditation. Put your attention at your heart center, take a few deep breaths, inhaling and exhaling, then use the mantra, "Open my heart." Ask any questions you desire and listen to the voice of your spirit speaking to you.

Allow yourself to be filled with divine love as it emerges from the depths of your soul. While being open to receive love, you become a channel for love.

I listen to the guidance of spirit
speaking through my heart.

SET HEALTHY BOUNDARIES

*"You know, you actually have the power to
choose to leave your unlocked cage. Release yourself
to create a life that you love!"*

– MICHELLE LEWIS

Establish healthy energetic boundaries with family members,
friends, coworkers, and even strangers to disengage from any
unwanted energies. You may have taken on the emotions of
others or even felt drained of energy in the presence of such
"energy bullies." This energetic drain can make you vulnerable
to compassion fatigue.

The more you set healthy boundaries, the less vulnerable you will
be to the energies of others. Set healthy boundaries by opening
your heart compassionately to others, but not taking on their
unhealthy processes or energies.

I am more loving and
compassionate when I set healthy
energetic boundaries.

LET YOUR SOUL SHINE THROUGH

"It's so clear that you have to cherish everyone. I think that's what I get from these older women, that every soul is to be cherished, that every flower is to bloom."

– ALICE WALKER

Meraki is a Greek word used to describe what happens when you leave your energetic signature—your soul, creativity, or love—in your work. It inspires having a passion for what you do every day and feeling connected with everyone who shares the experience with you. This energetic exchange is key to nurturing your creativity, fostering your spiritual growth, and enhancing your life.

Put your heart and soul into what you do, then love and joy will follow. Let your soul shine through your endeavors and into your relationships.

I put my heart and soul
into everything I do, and love
and joy follow.

SHINE FROM WITHIN

"Your anxiety lets you know what unresolved issues need to be healed and what feelings need to be released. This healing and release process can lead to personal transformation and making healthy life changes."

– DR. DEBRA REBLE

Your true self is light, so there's no need to validate your worthiness through what you do. Accomplishments and achievements are wonderful, however, if you are to live authentically, it is the light of your being, not the work of your hands, that must shine forth beyond everything—for that is your connection to your divine source and the basis for your full self-expression in life.

I illuminate my light from within.

DIVINE SUPPORT

"Always go with the choice that scares you the most, because that's the one that is going to require the most from you."

– CAROLINE MYSS

Trust is a powerful energy that brings you into your present awareness and moves you beyond fear. You activate it in moments when you experience anxiety and move forward regardless of your fear. When you tap into this heart-centered energy and make courageous choices, you shift from fear to faith by making leaps of trust.

Absolute trust in yourself is developed by practicing leaps of trust, one moment at a time. Strengthen your trust muscles by focusing on the positive events that have happened in your life—the moments where you took a leap of trust and all worked out well.

I trust that I am safe and divinely supported in the space between when I leap and when I land.

PRACTICE MINDFULNESS

*"You move totally away from reality when you believe
that there is a legitimate reason to suffer."*

– BYRON KATIE

Practice mindfulness by becoming an observer without judgment of your own thoughts, feelings, and sensations. Find a comfortable place where you won't be distracted. Take a few slow, deep breaths. Now imagine your mind as a vast, blue sky and your thoughts as white, billowy clouds. Watch as your thoughts move across your mind as clouds move across the sky. Now let go of your thoughts without judging, analyzing, or getting caught up in them.

Mindfully observe your thoughts five minutes a day and gradually build up to fifteen minutes every day. You can do this while walking and then extend it to other forms of movement as well.

I mindfully observe my thoughts
without judgment.

SPIRITUAL GROWTH

"Not everyone will recognize your true value and perfection, but you are exactly who you are supposed to be in exactly the right place for this moment!"

– JAMI HEARN

Opening your heart in gratitude brings you to grace. Before you get out of bed in the morning, put your hand on your heart, and name five things you are grateful for. The energy of gratitude will immediately drop you into your heart space, expand your present awareness, and set a positive tone for your day.

Appreciating what shows up in your life, especially your challenges, raises your vibration, which generates more positive energy to come back to you. Opening your heart in gratitude tunes your energy to a higher vibration of love.

I am grateful for the challenging situations in my life that support me to spiritually grow.

 MAY 2

GROUNDING YOUR ENERGIES

*"Advice is what we ask for when we already
know the answer but wish we didn't."*

– ERICA JONG

Calm and center yourself by grounding your energies. This is
especially helpful when you experience anxiety because your
energy collects around the top of your head. When you're
ungrounded, you may feel disoriented, discombobulated, and
often detached from your body.

To ground yourself, breathe deeply, touch the center of your chest,
and open your heart. You also can begin at the top of your head
and direct your energy down through your body to your feet.
This can work when you take a walk, stand, or lie on the grass.

I ground my energies so that
I remain calm and centered.

YOUR TRUE POWER

"The art of positive choices helps you to create the life you want. Life is a series of additions and subtractions. You control the calculator."

– GAIL MCMEEKIN

Recognize that you are your own power source. Your true power originates from within, from your heart, and initiates your reality. As a co-creator, wield this power to make inspired choices and stop relinquishing your power to others or your circumstances.

Trust your divine connection to source, and become aware of this unlimited creative energy flowing through you. Channel it to support the fullest expression of yourself, others, and the planet.

I wield my creative power
and channel it to support my
fullest expression.

PLAY WITH THE POSSIBILITIES

"Courage allows us to acknowledge our hurts, wounds, and imperfections without escaping, distracting or resisting them."

– DR. DEBRA REBLE

Take time to "just be." Give yourself permission to do the things that make your heart sing and your inner being come alive. Make the discerning choices that align with your heart and set your spirit free. Play with all the possibilities, dance in the light, and fully express who you are.

I don't need anyone's permission to fully express the light of my being.

MANIFEST YOUR VISION

"Embrace the constant cycle of change. Embrace each moment for what it is... beautiful."

– ISABELLA ROSE

Visualize yourself walking through life happy, enthusiastic, and fully alive. Write down this vision of your life as you see it now, as you hope it will be in six months, and how you would like it to be in five years. Then choose three steps you can take now toward manifesting your vision. Now, do them.

Today I take three steps toward creating the vision I see for my life.

RELATIONSHIP LIFE CYCLES

*"When we do the best we can, we never know what
miracle is wrought in our life, or in the life of another."*

– HELEN KELLER

Like the life cycles you move through as the years unfold,
relationships also have life cycles. Some last for only a brief
period and others a season or a lifetime. There are relationships
that show up to support your spiritual growth at particular
periods in your life.

Soul-hearted relationships transcend all life cycles and last a
lifetime. These are the rare people who accept your strengths
and weaknesses, are honest with you, love you unconditionally,
and reflect your true being. Such lifelong soul companions
make up your energetic soul support team.

I let go of the relationships that are
no longer appropriate to my being
at this time in my life.

CLEAR YOUR ENERGY FIELD

"The more anger towards the past you carry in your heart, the less capable you are of loving in the present."

– BARBARA DE ANGELIS

You can be easily triggered by other people's emotions and energies. When you feel a physical or emotional reaction, pause and say to yourself, "If this is mine, I will deal with it." If it's not, your energy field has been invaded, and you need to clear it. This old adage applies here, "Not my circus, not my monkeys." You can clear your energy field and release any negative energy by taking a shower or bath.

When it's yours, create the time and space to have a sacred chat with your emotional reaction. Lean into your deepest fears and vulnerabilities. See what needs to be healed.

I clear my energy field of
anything that is not mine.

WORTHY OF LOVE

"To be courageous is to lead with your heart, and embrace your truth, your inner thoughts, feelings, and experiences. It dares you to fully express who you are."

- DR. DEBRA REBLE

Release your shame and realize that you are worthy of love. This begins with embracing your vulnerabilities and connecting with the fragmented, unloved parts of yourself.

But before you can heal—before you can love and connect to yourself—you need to acknowledge that there are messy, imperfect parts of yourself.

I embrace my "perfect" imperfections.

BLESS THEIR JOURNEY

*"When we choose to treat ourselves with kindness
and compassion, we teach others by our self-nurturing example,
and the ripple effects are endless."*

– KELLEY GRIMES, MSW

Separating your reactions from someone else's gives you the healthy detachment you need to stop taking their reactions personally or blaming them for yours. Remain compassionate and responsive by reminding yourself that the other person is going through their own process of self-discovery, which likely has nothing to do with you. Trust that they are on their own soul's journey, and are creating the scenarios they need to spiritually transform.

I bless the other person
and their journey, which is separate
from my own.

BE WITH THE PAIN

*"Faith is knowing that after we have done what we can,
there is a turning over, a letting go, a trusting beyond
our knowing that relieves us."*

– ANNE WILSON SCHAEF

The more you lean into your vulnerabilities and release your pain, the more open you are to personal transformation. Your unhealed pain keeps you living in habitual ways and inhibits you from co-creating a fulfilling and happy life.

In order to heal, you need to spend time alone so you can confront your vulnerabilities—feelings of unworthiness or lovelessness. Be with whatever unresolved pain or wounds surface and expose them to the light. Gaining this awareness can be scary, or make you feel uncomfortable so be gentle and kind to yourself.

I embrace my vulnerabilities and
expose them to the light.

GRACE IN MOTION

"Anything you want to ask a teacher, ask yourself, and wait for the answer in silence."

– BYRON KATIE

Living in the flow of love is grace in motion. You have a sense of riding the crest of a wave, dancing in the light, and being aligned with your soul's journey. There is a natural lightheartedness and a sense that nothing is more important than the present moment. There are no obstacles to shining your light.

Laughter comes easily, as does flexibility in playing with all the possibilities in life. The more you live in the flow of love, the more you are a force of universal love for the good of all humanity.

I am grace in motion.

SUPPORTIVE RELATIONSHIPS

*"Life is not measured by the number of breaths we take,
but by the moments that take our breath away."*

– MAYA ANGELOU

Relationships provide you with the most opportunities for self-realization. They inspire you to spiritually progress beyond what you can achieve alone. When both people are actively pursuing their own spiritual paths, they offer each other a commitment to be the best they can be.

Begin a new relationship, whether it be a romance, friendship, or other, that is spiritually aligned, connected, and meaningful. Let go of any relationships that no longer serve or support you during this period in your life. Let yourself be open and vulnerable with this person so you can emotionally and spiritually grow.

I am open to new relationships that support me to be the best I can be.

LOVE TRANSCENDS FEAR

*"We do not have a sole purpose but instead
a soul purpose, which encompasses a multitude of passions
that inspire purposeful living."*

– DR. DEBRA REBLE

By loving yourself, you can change the world. You become a conduit for love when you fully embrace and express your true nature—which is, and always has been, love. The more you love yourself, the more you eliminate fear and negativity, connect compassionately with others, and become a love ambassador.

Love transcends fear every time. You can facilitate a positive shift in human consciousness by transcending negativity and ascending to the soul of love. You can do this by not reacting from fear but, instead, connect to a divine source through your heart.

When I love myself,
I change the world.

POSITIVE AND PRESENT

*"We must accept and love who we once were, so we can
fully embrace the future and all of its possibilities.
Step into the unknown and be yourself!"*

– KATHLEEN GUBITOSI, MA

When you live in the flow of love, you are a love ambassador.
You aren't a saint, prophet, or guru who maintains an austere
and monastic lifestyle. Quite the opposite, you live what seems
like everyday life. You usually go unnoticed until others realize
how happy, joyful, and peaceful you are, even in the midst of
life's messiness.

When others interact with you, they see how positive and present
you are compared to most people living at lower levels of spiritual
awareness. They feel completely seen and heard in your presence
because you acknowledge them with your heart and soul.

Every day I strive to be
a love ambassador.

ABUNDANCE MINDSET

"Words are medicine for what ails you, and the fuel
to take you where you want to go!"

– CRYSTAL COCKERHAM

So that abundance can flow freely, let go of the mindset that you deserve to receive gifts based on the gifts you give. Sustaining a flow of abundance doesn't depend on a credit and debit spreadsheet. It is produced by generously sharing your time, energies, and resources with others.

Give a gift, pay a bill, or offer to assist someone without any expectations or conditions. This keeps the energy in positive circulation. You create abundance when you give for the sake of giving, share for the sake of sharing, and love for the sake of loving, no strings attached.

I am open to the abundant
energy of the universe.

THROUGH THE EYES OF A CHILD

"Bringing the energy of nature into our homes will increase our sense of peace and harmony, will uplift our energy and promote a sense of wellbeing."

– FELICIA D'HAITI

Love comes naturally to children as it once did to you. Children don't think about expressing love, they just do it. Open and optimistic, they trust their innate ability to love and be loved. Above all, they radiate love without ego, expectations, or reservations. They show you that nothing is more important than being love.

Spend the day with a four-year-old and you will again know love. Children are your best teachers for how to love and lead with your heart. See yourself reflected in the love-light of a child and you will know without a doubt that love is who you are.

Through the eyes of a child,
I see my reflection as love.

WITH EVERY BREATH

"Opening our hearts creates a flow of abundance that stands alone, separate from any and all conditions. It is an energetic gift in and of itself which brings us blessings a million times over."

– DR. DEBRA REBLE

Practicing deep, slow, intentional breathing can draw more oxygen into your body, reduce anxiety, and restore balance to your nervous system. A regular deep breathing practice can help you remain calm in stressful situations.

Put your hand on your heart and focus on your breath. On your inhale, count up to five seconds as you breathe in, and on your exhale draw your breath out for another five seconds. Do this until your breathing is rhythmic, and you feel calm and centered. Then, for at least a minute, open your heart and let your energies expand outward in gratitude for yourself or someone else.

I breathe in love and breathe
out fear and anxiety.

MAY 18

INTENTIONAL THOUGHTS

*"To breathe deeply and honor yourself, to take a sacred pause,
contemplate and "just be" is a gift!"*

– CINDY HIVELY

Like a pebble dropped into a pond, your intention, in co-creation with your divine source, sets off an energetic vibration that radiates outward and shifts everything in your path. Your heart center generates a resonant field of light energy that can influence the thoughts, emotions, and actions of others and the world in a positive way.

Because any thought or spoken word functions as an intention, keep your thoughts and words positive. Let your intention reflect what you want rather than what you don't want. If you catch yourself speaking negatively, shift your thoughts and words to a more positive vibration.

I align my intentions with the
highest vibration in the universe.

RELEASE WORRY

*"Forget about the fast lane. If you really want to fly,
just harness your power to your passion."*

– OPRAH

To be fully present in your life, engage in a moment-to-moment awareness of what's happening around and within you. Pay attention to your experience without getting caught up in your thoughts. You no longer worry about the future or regret the choices you've made in the past.

The moment you form a thought about something, the event is already past. Since the present moment is all there is, celebrate it and then release it. When you do, you experience an overwhelming sense of joy and contentment, with no yearning, aching, or dissatisfaction to distract you from what is happening in the now.

I live peacefully without worrying
about the future or regretting
the past.

KEEPING YOUR ENERGY CLEAR

"It takes courage to be who we are in the world."

– DR. DEBRA REBLE

When you want to clear your energy field of negative energy, imagine the person or situation in pink light. Surround them with pink bubbles or pink clouds—whatever image works for you. At the same time, imagine yourself bathed in radiant white light. This clearing practice seals the negative energy away from you because the vibration of pink light governs the physical universe, short-circuiting and isolating negative energy.

You can also clear your energy field by taking a shower or bath. Bathe in Epsom or Himalayan sea salts to clear any unwanted or toxic energies you may have absorbed during the day.

I clear my energy field of any toxic
or negative energy from the day.

HIGHER–VIBE RELATIONSHIPS

"I believe avoidance comes down to fear. Of change.
Of failure. That's how our ego keeps us 'safe.' Lean into
fear and trust all will be well."

– DEBORAH KEVIN

Letting go of a relationship can be challenging especially
when that person has been in your life for a long time. But
you can release with love, and in appreciation for the purpose
the relationship has served in your life. Maintaining unhealthy
relationships drains your life force energy while letting go of
them creates space.

Blessing and releasing unhealthy relationships with loving
compassion and integrity teaches you how to forgive your past,
heal yourself, and unleash a flow of positive energy through
your heart. This love energy will attract healthy soul-hearted
relationships in the future.

I let go of unhealthy relationships
which create the space for healthy
soul-hearted ones.

WISDOM OF THE HEART

*"Sometimes we have to be the soul that actually strikes
the match to light the fire of change. Have the courage to strike
the match yourself. Be bold!"*

– AMY JOHNSON

When you listen to your heart, you discover that you are love.
You become a conduit for transmitting and receiving divinely
inspired information. This not only awakens you to your
authentic self but leads to self-healing.

Listening to your heart opens up an intimate relationship with
yourself. You receive assistance with daily challenges, waste
less time and energy being anxious about life's difficulties, and
experience a divine encounter with yourself. It leads to a more
spiritual way of life, giving you more peace of mind.

When I listen to my heart,
I discover I am love.

EMBRACE FORGIVENESS

"We are not held back by the love we didn't receive in the past, but by the love we're not extending in the present."

– MARIANNE WILLIAMSON

The practice of forgiveness creates new space for positive energy to return to you and opens your heart to love. Your heart is an energetic clearinghouse that transforms any hurt, grievance, or resentment into loving compassion. By forgiving and letting go, you make the past powerless over your life.

Forgiveness renews your connection to others, enhances empathy, and clears any negative emotions. Some journal questions to facilitate this practice include: Who in your life have you not forgiven? How does this interfere with your life? How can you forgive this person now?

When I forgive, I make the past powerless over my life.

COMPASSIONATE COVENANT

"By honoring our needs for personal time and engaging in activities that restore and inspire us, we have more energy and stamina to energetically serve others. Take time for yourself."

– DR. DEBRA REBLE

Taking time for precious self-care is essential to enhancing your body, mind, and spirit. It increases your energy, brings peace of mind, and restores inner balance. Setting aside time each day to nurture yourself can help you reduce stress, calm your nervous system, and feel renewed.

Make a compassionate covenant with yourself. Practice small acts of loving-kindness toward yourself as you go through your day. Make a special meal, leave Post-It love notes on the bathroom mirror, buy yourself flowers, or plan a self-care retreat.

Today I take precious care of myself by practicing small acts of kindness.

SAVOR THE MOMENTS

"You don't need validation or permission to pursue your passions. You know best what you want your life story to look like and what you're capable of."

– DR. COLLEEN GEORGES

Carve out a few moments each day to consciously focus on, and identify a positive experience you had that day. Take a moment and reflect on a recent experience, large or small, that made you feel joyful or happy. Something may have made you smile or laugh, or a nice surprise may have come your way. Whatever it is, give yourself a moment to visualize it.

Now let yourself experience the feeling you had when it happened. Feel it in your entire body. Notice the change in you as you savor this moment. Let yourself deeply appreciate the deliciousness of this feeling.

I savor the positive moments
in my life.

LET GO OF PERFECTION

*"Our conditioning will tell us we are not enough.
Our inner goddess tells us otherwise. Which voice we
listen to IS our choice."*

– MARCIA MARINER

Let go of the need to make the "perfect" choice. The pattern of perfectionism can keep you feeling stuck and from making any choice at all. When you feel fearful of making a wrong choice, remember that you can always choose again.

Don't judge yourself for having made a wrong choice. Instead, view your so-called mistakes as opportunities for transformation. Trust that they will steer you in a new direction and give you the information you need to make a course correction.

I let go of making the "perfect" choice
and make choices that align
with my heart.

COMPASSIONATE DETACHMENT

*"Facing our deepest vulnerabilities allows us to recognize and uproot
the negative beliefs, unhealthy patterns, and unresolved pain that
inhibit us from living an abundant, joyful and balanced life."*

– DR. DEBRA REBLE

Practice compassionate detachment by observing others'
processes without getting invested or entangled in them. When
you open your heart, withhold judgment, and remain nonreactive,
you experience any challenging situation from a spiritually
elevated perspective. This gives you a healthy detachment as well
as the capacity to feel compassion for even those who deceive or
hurt you.

Pause frequently and become aware by breathing and focusing on
your heart center. Clear any reaction by saying, "Open and let go,
or let it be." This way, you remain compassionate, but disengaged
from any negative process.

I compassionately detach myself from
others' unhealthy processes.

THE KEY TO JOY

"If you have only one smile in you, give it to the people you love.
Don't be surly at home, then go out in the street and start grinning
'Good morning' at total strangers."

– MAYA ANGELOU

Sustaining a positive mindset is key to well-being, happiness, and joy no matter what's happening in your life. Looking on the bright side of life governs how you perceive and respond to life's challenges. It helps you to go with the flow and handle any challenge with ease, grace, and responsiveness.

Begin to think positively even if you do not feel that way at the time. You need to have three times more positive than negative thoughts to create a positive shift in your thinking. When a negative thought pops up, you can say, "Bless and release, or cancel, cancel," and then replace it with a positive one.

I consciously shift my negative
thoughts to positive ones.

IN EVERY MOMENT

"Doing something each day that gives you your 'oxygen' is a sure-fire way to increase your level of joy."

– KELLY MISHELL

In every relationship, in every moment, you can choose love. The more you express love toward others, the more you see that you are lovable, and discover how to love more intimately. Being lovingly connected to others brings out the best in you, allows you to connect emotionally, and spiritually grow.

All relationships are opportunities to open and connect at the heart level. It is a true gift to yourself to connect with others, as they amplify the love already present within you. To attract loving and connected relationships, you must embody the love and connection you seek.

I open my heart and express love in every encounter and attract loving and connected relationships.

SPIRITUAL RESPONSIBILITY

*"Perched on the seat of her soul, she radiated self-love
that illuminated through her skin emanating vibrations
that encouraged others to do the same."*

– HEATHER MARIA

It's time to take responsibility for your life and not relinquish
your power to forces outside yourself. Just hearing the word
"responsibility" can feel heavy, even daunting. Yet, spiritual
responsibility is the responsibility you have to co-create the divine
life you want. This means being responsible for your intentions
and the choices that you can make to manifest them.

Choice is a powerful tool when you are accountable for your life.
Start by making more inspired choices by asking questions such
as, "Who do you want to be in relationships? What do you want
to create? Where to do you want to live?" Step up, trust yourself,
and handle whatever is positively happening in your life.

I am accountable for
co-creating my divine life.

YOUR DIVINE LEGACY

"The best and most beautiful things in the world cannot be seen nor touched but are felt in the heart."

– HELEN KELLER

Leaving a legacy of love begins with positive energy and a healthy optimism for your future and the future of your world. When you channel love and create what you want in alignment with what is best for yourself, others, and your world, this flow becomes a spiritual path that leads to living joyfully, abundantly, and well. Leaving a legacy of love is the path of seeing life as a challenge, an adventure and, most of all, a gift.

Being and expressing love is your divine legacy and your purpose in being here on earth.

I leave a legacy of love by being and expressing love.

FREE TO EXPRESS YOURSELF

"When someone shows you who they are, believe them the first time."

– MAYA ANGELOU

Soul-hearted relationships create a safe environment for love. You feel free to express yourself, knowing that your hopes and dreams will be accepted. Each person assists the other in growing spiritually and living in congruence with their soul's journey.

In such a relationship, you are celebrated for who you are. With such energetic support, you have the freedom to pursue your passions, follow your heart, and fully express yourself. Like popcorn, the kernels of your soul's potential are able to burst forth through the nurturing of each other's being.

I create soul-hearted relationships
in which I feel safe to express
my true being.

AN ENERGETIC SAFE HAVEN

*"Leaning into our vulnerabilities requires spending time alone
so we can confront the source of those vulnerabilities—our feelings
of unworthiness or disconnection—and stand face to face
with whatever unresolved pain surfaces."*

– DR. DEBRA REBLE

Create an energetically safe haven of love with a friend or partner
to venture into deeper intimacy. Be fully present by maintaining
eye contact, listening without interruption, and refraining from
offering your opinion until invited.

Respond to their sharing by repeating back to them what you
heard them say. Even when you feel uncomfortable, open your
heart, and accept what they say as their truth. In this safe space,
let your guard down, allow your feelings to surface, and then,
when it's your turn, share with the other person.

I create a safe haven to encourage intimacy in my relationships.

CLEARING THE PAST

"Learn to get in touch with the silence within yourself and know that everything in this life has a purpose. There are no mistakes, no coincidences, all events are blessings given to us to learn from."

– ELIZABETH KÜBLER-ROSS

Clearing the energy of the past is a healthy process akin to sloughing off dead skin cells that can accumulate and block the growth of new, healthy cells. Animals, birds, and plants also move through a regenerative clearing process—cycles of shedding, molting, or loss of leaves—as a part of their natural development.

Similarly, as you shed the layers of your past, you initiate a cycle of transformation that leads to spiritual growth. To move forward in your life, embrace this natural shedding process. Clear your life of anyone or anything that doesn't align with your vision of well-being and happiness.

I clear the energy of the past
to initiate transformation.

EVALUATE YOUR RELATIONSHIPS

*"Every time we stretch ourselves out of our comfort zone
and take inspired action toward our dreams we discover something
magical and expansive waiting on the other side."*

– LINDA JOY

Evaluate your relationships to see who's on your energetic soul support team by asking yourself, "Who unconditionally loves and supports me to spiritually grow and reach my fullest potential? Who is trustworthy, has integrity, and is impeccable with their word? Who accepts me for who I am, but gives loving feedback when asked? Who brings out the best in me?" If you answer "no" to any of these questions, then this person is not on your soul team.

Surround yourself with people who are loving, trustworthy, and who are committed to their own personal growth.

I surround myself with people who
love, support, and encourage me
to spiritually grow.

HONOR YOUR INNER LIGHT

*"You'll never know who you are unless you
shed who you pretend to be."*

– VIRONIKA TUGALEVA

If you are fixated on how others perceive you and try to live up
to their expectations, you are not being true to yourself. Do not
live in fear of making a mistake, failing, or disappointing them
because you desperately want their approval. Such behavior only
diminishes your sense of self-worth, limits your ability to make
your own choices, and undermines trust in yourself.

There is nothing enlightened about shrinking yourself so that
others feel secure or fulfilled. You no longer need to sacrifice
your worthiness to make other people feel comfortable. Let go
of what others think, open to your true self, and show up fully in
your light.

I let go of what others' think
and step into my light.

A POINT OF BALANCE

*"When you truly love yourself, you do not envy the
good fortune of others but trust that there is enough
love and abundance to go around."*

– DR. DEBRA REBLE

In all of your relationships, find a point of balance between
supporting the needs of the other person and your own. When
you fail to satisfy your own needs, it results in no one's needs
being fulfilled. Such a hyper-focus on giving to others without
receiving can create an energetic and emotional imbalance in
your relationships.

Although it's wonderful to serve others, in your need to give,
you can become overly responsible or overly cooperative. This
tendency to over-help can lead to a pattern of codependency
where you focus on other people's lives. Let go of your need to
be needed and celebrate your worth coming from who you are,
not what you do.

I let go of the pattern of
codependency in my relationships.

CULTIVATE SELF-LOVE

*"When we are able to see the choices we make through
the eyes of self-acceptance, we are transformed."*

– JODI LIVON

Wake up in the morning loving yourself even when you feel tired, uninspired, or depressed. Focus on the aspects of yourself that you love rather than those you dislike. Stop berating, shaming, or beating yourself up with negative self-talk.

As you move through your day, notice any self-deprecating thoughts or words, and replace them with positive affirmations such as, "I am kind, I am generous, or I am trustworthy." Imagine how one moment of self-compassion could change your day. Now consider how such moments repeated over and over could change your life.

I cultivate a climate of self-love
with loving self-talk.

CONSCIOUSLY CLEAR YOUR LIFE

"I have noticed that the Universe loves Gratitude. The more Grateful you are, the more goodies you get."

– LOUISE L. HAY

Consciously scan your living environment and notice where any possible energy blocks may exist. If something catches your attention, pause, and sense if this item resonates with you. If it doesn't, give it away to someone else or discard it. Keep the things you cherish and let go of the rest.

The purging of physical clutter goes hand in hand with the clearing of emotional clutter. Engage in energetic feng shui by noticing what still serves and resonates with you at this time. Clear your life of anything that does not align with your well-being and future intentions. This clearing process will open up new space and energy to bring in more of what you want.

I consciously clear anything that does not resonate with my life at this time.

INVITE MIRACLES IN

*"Recovering from failure is a process. There are no time limits.
Just be sure to not give up."*

– MICHELLE LEMOI

Your spiritual resilience makes it possible not only to endure
hardship and suffering but to use any challenging situation
for spiritual growth. Your spirit is stronger than any situation
you encounter and can transcend even the most devastating
circumstances in your life.

Rise above whatever is happening in your life no matter how
difficult. View problems or obstacles as stepping stones for
change. This helps you remain open and flexible as your day
unfolds. With such resilience, you invite miracles into your life.

My spirit is stronger than any
situation I may face.

THE LAW OF LOVE

"Spiritual resiliency is the foundation for being love, happiness, and peace in the world. The more we tune in to the guidance of our spirits, the more we are led to a spiritually attuned life."

– DR. DEBRA REBLE

You radiate love when you open your heart to yourself, other people, and life itself. A person who loves sends out a high-frequency vibration into the world, while someone who has difficulty loving emits a lower frequency. The spiritual law of attraction, which is also the law of love, suggests that the energy you radiate expands and attracts more of the same energy in return.

As a love conduit, you circulate loving energy through your positive thoughts, feelings, and choices, benefiting yourself and others. This energetic attraction guides you to think, speak, feel, or act, and is the direct link to your soul.

I radiate love and attract love to me in every area of my life.

THE POWER OF AWARENESS

*"Your inner child has been waiting all your life for you
to own your power and play, co-creating with the universe,
expanding it with your love."*

– TONIA BROWNE

Conscious awareness is your intuitive ability to tune in to information that gives you a broader spiritual perspective. Such awareness bypasses logical thinking and awakens an inner knowing through your heart. This allows you to notice, appreciate, and pay attention to your thoughts, feelings, and sensations in the present moment.

The power of awareness gives you access to a greater wealth of information to support your spiritual growth and well-being. Such higher awareness overrides any negative thoughts and allows you to tune in to your spirit to guide you.

My unbounded awareness opens
me to spiritual information
that guides my life.

ENLIGHTENED CHOICES

"It's all about taking personal responsibility for your own happiness, keeping life in perspective, and being gentler with yourself and others while accessing your inner peace and wisdom."

– KRISTINE CARLSON

When you make inspired choices, you choose what soulfully aligns with you, and what does not. You make the conscious choices that not only sustain your well-being, but also the well-being of the planet and all its inhabitants.

Each enlightened choice you make from your heart serves you as well as others' highest and greatest good. When you make choices from your heart, you perpetuate a more universal, encompassing, and loving worldview.

I make enlightened choices from my heart that align with universal love.

ACTS OF KINDNESS

"Brave are the courageous souls who dare step outside the predefined yellow-brick road."

– KAMI GUILDNER

Every act of kindness and compassion raises the vibration of the universe. These are powerful forces that generate a harmonic convergence of love. The more kind and compassionate you are with yourself, the more you can be so with others. The inverse is also true. You may be so busy wanting to be loved that you fail to see where you can give love. Yet, it is in giving love through care, assistance, and acts of kindness that you receive its' benefits.

Give and receive love without expectations, conditions, or obligations. Be kind whenever possible, and you will find that you will feel more positive, open, and loving.

I am kind and compassionate with myself and love flows out to others and the world.

LET GO AND FORGIVE

"Time may ease the pain of loss, but it's being fully present with our heartbreak that leads to healing."

– DR. DEBRA REBLE

The healing power of forgiveness promotes well-being because it helps you release negative feelings and replace them with positive ones. Forgiving a person for the harm they caused you and, likewise, making amends for hurting someone are positive acts that sustain loving connected relationships

As a practice, forgiveness clears negative emotions which when unreleased may create energy blocks in your body. It also frees you from your past and opens an energetic space for you to create a better future. If you want to love and to be loved, you must let go and forgive.

Through forgiveness, I let go
of negative emotions that block
the flow of love.

THE PATH OF TRUTH

"You yourself, as much as anybody in the entire universe, deserve your love and affection."

– SHARON SALZBERG

The path of truth supports your integrity. Like the links in a chain, integrity is the strength that holds you to a higher spiritual level. Integrity aligns your thoughts, words, and actions with a divine flow of energy.

Stay true to yourself and your word. Your spoken and unspoken words are powerful intentions to the universe. They need to be consciously chosen and lovingly expressed. Be impeccable with your word, and you will be seen as trustworthy.

When I am impeccable with my word,
I strengthen my integrity.

JOYFUL ABANDON

"You get in life what you have the courage to ask for."

– OPRAH

Lightheartedness includes spontaneity, humor, and play—all launchpads to creativity and spiritual growth. Being light-hearted liberates the mind, opens the heart, and lifts the spirit. You take life less seriously, see it as a passionate adventure to be enjoyed, and stay as flexible as possible.

Align with your soul's passion and purpose and sustain joy in your life. Spend time playing, being spontaneous, and taking pleasure in the simple things in life that make your heart sing with joyful abandon.

I live with lightheartedness
and joyful abandon.

HOLD SPACE FOR LOVE

*"When you find joy in everything you do, you will
be living your highest purpose."*

– YAELLE SCHWARCZ

Set healthy energetic boundaries before entering any difficult
or challenging situation. The simple act of opening your heart
and radiating love energy outward raises your vibration and the
vibration of those around you. Let love beam out from you
creating an expansive energy field that fills the room.

Like a divine light shield, this energetic boundary protects you
from any negativity or unwanted energy that may be coming at
you. By opening your heart and beaming love, you hold the space
for love to shift any negativity.

When I radiate love, I create
an energetic boundary that protects
me from negativity.

CELEBRATE YOUR DIVINITY

"It's okay if it scares you. Just don't let it stop you."

– SUSAN WILKING HORAN

Celebrate your divine being every day, especially during your birthday month. Create your birthday month in any way you want. Let this sacred time commemorate the divine choice you made to come into this physical life. Take time to honor the ending of one life cycle and the opening of a new one with endless possibilities.

As your birthday month begins, reflect on the previous year. See which intentions have manifested and which ones need to be tweaked or changed. Write down your new intentions to set the tone for new beginnings.

I celebrate my divine being every day.

WATCHING FOR SPIRITUAL SIGNS

"When we create an energetic support team, we invite into our lives people who love us unconditionally, without judging, enabling, or interfering with our choices."

– DR. DEBRA REBLE

When you shift to a less hurried pace, you become more consciously aware. You see the spiritual signs and hear the whisper of spirit through your heart. These are the spiritual breadcrumbs that guide you through the enchanted forest of your life so that you can make the most discerning choices possible.

Your heightened awareness is enhanced when you slow down and make yourself available to inspired information. Being fully present, you see that spirit acts in straightforward ways so you can recognize the signs it gives you.

I slow my pace to be more consciously aware of spiritual signs.

PRACTICE HIGHER AWARENESS

*"What if the journey is not about becoming
a better version of yourself, but rather remembering
the perfection of who you are."*

– LIZETE MORAIS

When feeling things deeply and compassionately is your
superpower, practice higher awareness instead of over-awareness.
Put your attention at your heart center to bring yourself into
higher awareness. Here you can align your mind and heart, which
bypasses the over-awareness of your brain. This allows you to
feel, sense, and intuit freely.

Take a media break to reduce over-awareness. Limit the amount
of time you spend watching the news or surfing the internet. This
applies to people, too, so consciously consider with whom and
where you spend your time.

In every moment I choose to tap
into my higher awareness.

TRUST GUIDANCE OF SPIRIT

*"I can honestly say that I was never affected by the question
of the success of an undertaking. If I felt it was the right thing to do,
I was for it regardless of the possible outcome."*

– GOLDA MEIR

Lead with your heart and then use your head. When you bypass your thoughts, you become open to receiving spiritual information through your heart. You notice the information that comes from spirit whether it's a gut feeling, an "a-ha" moment, or an inner knowing. Above all, you see, sense, and intuit what is in alignment with your soul's journey.

By focusing on your heart and bringing your attention there, you move into present awareness. And with awareness comes the ability to lead with your heart and trust the guidance of spirit. This is where compassion, acceptance, and trust in yourself and your divine source live.

I lead with my heart, trusting
the guidance of spirit.

DROP INTO YOUR HEART

"Open your thoughts to the probability that you are more intuitive than you realize."

– SYLVIA CLARE

It's not easy remaining calm in the center of a storm raging around you. When fear or chaos arrives, and you feel yourself spinning out with anxiety, tap into your heart and trust that all is well no matter what is happening around you.

Trusting yourself when you're in the midst of fear can be challenging. But within every storm, there is a peaceful center and that center is trust—trust of yourself in connection with your divine source. Drop into your heart space and find that center of inner peace within you. Use the information you receive to spiritually guide you.

I trust that I can weather any storm and find my peaceful center.

KEEP AN OPEN HEART

"We attract love by being love."

– DR. DEBRA REBLE

Open your heart more than ever before and allow yourself to experience love in ways you may not have been capable of in the past. Instead of operating from fear, awaken to the power of love within you which transcends all limiting thoughts and beliefs.

Knowing that you are love will profoundly heal you. So much so that you become a conduit for the expression of love with yourself, loved ones, and the world. And, since unity and duality coexist, you can experience unconditional love in a conditional world.

I keep an open heart which
sustains unconditional love in
a conditional world.

BRING IT TO THE LIGHT

*"When it is time, we walk the corridors of our heart,
letting go of the shattered threads of once-believed dreams.
We forgive and find a new spring."*

– GWENDOLYN M. PLANO

Transformation involves spiritual growth, and such growth requires healing your psychic pain. Sometimes an unexpected situation can trigger the exposure of an unhealed emotional wound. Even when you think you have worked through the pain, you may find yourself circling back to heal even deeper layers of the trauma.

Like motion sensors, your physical and emotional reactions alert you to where there is unresolved pain. These subtle cues tell you to pause, check in with yourself, and notice what needs to be healed. But, you have to tune in and listen. Then you can bring this unhealed pain into the light and release it.

I tune in and listen to my body
to heal my unresolved pain.

DARE TO SHINE

"Expecting and receiving joyance is guaranteed by writing an AAA List—Always Appreciating in Advance List.™"

– LORE RAYMOND

It is time to claim sovereignty over your life. Time to stop compromising yourself by continuing to play small or hiding in the shadows. You are to here to live an authentic life and fulfill your soul's purpose. Affirm that you are strong, capable, and worthwhile and don't need anyone's permission to be or express yourself.

When you want to shrink, open your heart and shine your light. Because when your light shines bright, others can see your essence, take a step forward, and light the path for those behind them. You are divinely supported to transcend anything that limits you and your brilliance. Be courageous and allow the truth of who you are to shine through your heart.

I dare to be seen, heard, and acknowledged as the light I am.

YOUR HEART KNOWS

*"Sometimes it is just about taking the first step,
only then can greatness find us."*

– COLLEEN MARIOTTI

Listen to others, respect their points of view, and sort out what works for you and what doesn't. Keep in mind that it's just their opinion and doesn't mean it's right or wrong. When you disagree with someone, remain calm, tolerant, and non-reactive.

Always check with your heart any information you receive from external sources. Remind yourself that it is "just information" unless it resonates with what you know to be true for you. If it aligns with your truth, use it to guide you to make better and more meaningful choices.

It's "just information" unless it resonates with my heart as my truth.

SPIRITUAL SHIFTS

*"Success is liking yourself, liking what you do,
and liking how you do it."*

– MAYA ANGELOU

Transitions are passages which bring about spiritual shifts.
While in a transition, hold steady, open your heart, and trust
yourself no matter if you lose your glasses, your balance, your
job, or a friend. You may feel as if the grids beneath your feet
are shifting and your internal landscape is recalibrating. It's all
happening in preparation for you to step into your light and
fulfill your soul's potential.

With any beginning, you are given the spiritual opportunity to
change direction, clear your path of anything that doesn't serve
you, and set new intentions of what truly does. Love and let go
of more in your life than ever before. Let go of your past to open
to new possibilities for your future.

I embrace transitions in my life
as spiritual shifts.

YOUR DIVINE ESSENCE

*"Inner wisdom is learning to observe yourself
and your energy. When you are in control of your energy,
you are in control of your life."*

– MICHELE GREER

Affirm your trust in a higher power (whatever that happens
to be for you) and connect to this divine source through your
heart. Sustaining this connection inspires new ideas, intuitions,
and information beyond the physical level. Open to your divine
essence in ways that truly express your heart.

These new ideas that enter your awareness source from spirit. Let
them guide you in your life rather than the way you think, believe,
or act from the past. It is the light of your being that shines forth
beyond everything—for that is your connection to your divine
source and your full self-expression.

I trust in myself and my divine source
as my security and my strength.

LISTEN WITH AN OPEN HEART

*"To be courageous is to lead with your heart,
and reveal your truth your inner thoughts, feelings,
and experiences honestly and openly."*

– DR. DEBRA REBLE

Practice compassionate detachment by opening your heart in loving compassion for the other person while simultaneously removing yourself from their unhealthy reactions or energies. This way you can still provide loving support, yet remain calm, nonreactive, and nonjudgmental.

When someone wants to vent their feelings with you, prepare to be a sounding board by listening with an open heart and establishing clear energetic boundaries. This way you refrain from taking on their negative processes, giving unsolicited advice, or trying to fix the situation.

I open my heart in compassion
while removing myself from others'
unhealthy energies.

TRUSTING YOUR CHOICES

*"When we surround ourselves with objects that support
our vision of who we are and who we are becoming,
we gain clarity and comfort in our life path."*

– FELICIA D'HAITI

Making a choice, even if it leads you down a different path, gives you new information to guide your life. You may have made a choice only to find out that you're not heading in the direction that you wanted to go. Don't judge yourself as having failed or made the wrong choice. Just realize that it put you on the path of where you really needed to be at that point in time.

Choice is a powerful tool to help you get unstuck or unblock your energy. Don't be afraid to make a decision for it frees you to make your dreams a reality. This is the energy of creation.

I make a choice knowing I can
always choose again.

TAKING HEALTHY BREAKS

*"See every obstacle as a teacher preparing you in ways
that book learning cannot. Say, 'thank you' for
the opportunity to learn and grow."*

– NETTIE OWENS

Taking healthy breaks throughout your day is key to enjoying a healthy and happy life. Breaks give your body and mind time to let go of stress and tension. When you allow yourself to rest and relax, you will feel more balanced and at peace. Your breaks can be as simple as closing your eyes and breathing deeply, taking a walk, or decompressing in solitude from your day.

Sometimes a moment to listen to music or meditate can be just what you need to let go and release anything from your day. Consider making today the start of taking healthy breaks to give yourself a chance to unwind and just be.

I take healthy breaks to give myself
what I need to rest and restore.

ALL RETURNS TO ME

*"It feels wonderful to love others. But I always remember
that it feels amazingly wonderful to love myself.
I am my own best friend."*

– LILIANA VANASCO

Practice loving-kindness, non-judgment, and acceptance of yourself and others. As you move through your day, keep an open heart and extend unconditional love to whomever you meet. You have the opportunity to "be the blessing," to be a divine presence of love.

In these moments, pay attention to the connection between your heart and the other person's. Then bless the individual in loving compassion. Opening your heart and radiating love to them helps you release resentment or judgment and more quickly forgive.

All that I am, do, and express
returns to me as love.

THE SACRED SPACE OF TRUST

"Live in the GIVE by sharing your treasure.
Never forget, 'You are the only YOU in the Universe.'"

– SUSAN KAY DAHL

Trust lays the groundwork for all intimate relationships. When you are in a mutually trusting relationship, you are free to express who you truly are. Creating an environment of trust with another person requires accepting yourself for who you are, the other person for who they are, and the relationship for what it is in the moment.

With trust in place, you know that the other person is always there, loving, and nurturing and will respond when needed. You draw strength and solace from the relationship without constantly having to question it. In the sacred space of trust, you can be vulnerable and still know you will be loved and cherished.

I trust myself, which gives me the
insight to know if someone
is trustworthy.

MANIFEST YOUR DESIRES

"The things that we hide, those shameful experiences, are what ultimately give us our superpowers. Shine the light in your dark corners and be grateful for all your experiences."

– DEBORAH KEVIN

Celebrate your freedom of spirit by making a choice to love, create, and live fully. Yield to this freedom by trusting that nothing matters except the present moment. Be inspired to break out of your comfort zones, make new choices, and expand your horizons.

Honor your independent spirit that knows no boundaries, sees beyond obstacles, and fully expresses itself. Let go of any self-imposed limits, knowing that your possibilities are endless. You will see the soul potential you have to realize your wildest dreams and that there is nothing you can't create or manifest!

I am free to manifest
my heart's desires.

RESTORE PEACE AND HARMONY

"There is nothing enlightened about 'shrink-wrapping'
ourselves so that others feel secure or fulfilled.
Live your truth and shine your light."

– DR. DEBRA REBLE

Let go of any grievances so that you open to the flow of love, and restore peace and harmony in your life. Try to clear any unresolved grievance and release any resentment as soon as it surfaces. Releasing resentment frees up your energy so you can redirect it positively toward creating a more fulfilling life.

Releasing unresolved grievances does not constitute a free-for-all to blame, attack, or criticize another. Rather, it is a respectful exchange of honest and loving feedback. Like the new saplings that emerge from the ashes of a forest fire, you can create a new form of relationship each time you let go of an old resentment or past hurt.

I let go of any grievances and heal
resentments that block the
flow of love.

SOUL BE IT

"When you face a new challenge, remember the skills, talent, guts and resources that got you through before."

– LYNN A. ROBINSON

Open your heart as a bridge between yourself and your soul. Like striking a tuning fork, you feel your energy elevating to this higher vibration. Take a moment and tap into your soul energy. Feel yourself channeling this divine energy through your heart and into your life. In this awakened space, you are open and connected to your soul's path.

Now visualize a path of white light before you—your soul's path. See yourself out in front of this path guiding your life into form as you've always imagined it. Visualize your intentions in alignment with your soul's path and see them unfold. Be here a moment and repeat the mantra, "Soul Be It."

My soul's path is unfolding as I've always imagined. Soul Be It.

A SAFE HAVEN OF LOVE

"Celebrate who you are in your deepest heart. Love yourself, and the world will love you."

– AMY LEIGH MERCREE

You may desire deeper levels of intimacy with yourself and your loved ones. Such meaningful relationships begin with feeling "safe" to openly share your vulnerable self. Open your heart, let down your guard, and allow yourself to be vulnerable with another person.

Create a safe haven of love in your relationships by loving yourself without qualification. When you feel inherently worthy of love, you become your own safe haven. This frees you to fully express who you are with friends, loved ones, and even strangers. Put your "heart" out there and support others to share their vulnerability and step into the space of intimacy with you.

I create a safe haven to share my vulnerability and step into intimacy with another.

SOUL-HEARTED PARTNERSHIPS

*"Knowing your purpose, from the depths of your soul,
and pursuing it passionately allows you to find greater
peace-of-mind and trust in your journey."*

– LAURA P. CLARK

The soul-hearted partnership is greater than the sum of its partners. A powerful flow of energy emanates from your unity of love, purpose, and being. It brings forth your talents and abilities to be used for your personal growth as well as for a higher spiritual calling.

Soul-hearted partners are comets weaving their combined energies in an alignment of purpose, passion, and intimacy. When these intertwining energies are fully expressed, you co-create a happy and fulfilling life that uplifts you and benefits others.

I am open to a
soul-hearted partnership.

LET GO OF CONTROL

"When you choose to focus on all the wonderful things about you, you'll stand taller and stronger as you boldly and authentically live your life."

– FELICIA BAUCOM

Tune into the flow of divine energy in your life and let go of your need to control every detail and situation. Instead, trust yourself and your connection with source and flow with ease and grace. While you may not be able to control other people or the situation, you can choose how you respond.

When you fully trust yourself and draw on this energy source, you co-create your own reality. Trust your connection to this source of creation, ignite your intentions, and open yourself to endless possibilities.

I let go of control and trust myself
and my divine source.

LOVE BEYOND EXPECTATIONS

"We need to find the courage to say no to the things and people that are not serving us if we want to rediscover ourselves and live our lives with authenticity."

– BARBARA DE ANGELIS

Let love be the motivation for everything you think, say, and do. When you express love beyond any expectations or conditions, your life will transform itself. Radiate love from your heart to everyone you encounter. Consciously live each moment with an open heart, a kind and compassionate spirit, and as stress-free as possible.

Celebrate each day no matter if the shopping line is long, the traffic is congested, or your interactions with people are more challenging. Remember any situation can be handled with love, humor, flexibility, and a sense of adventure.

I express unconditional love which transforms my life and the world.

THE SACRED SPACE TO HEAL

*"Keep working on your positive mindset and watching
the thoughts and words which create your actions and habits.
You will change your destiny."*

– ANN SANFELIPPO

Acknowledging the positive side to loss doesn't numb its pain,
for it is the pain itself that opens you to deeper love, trust, and
spiritual healing. The pain lets you know to take time to sit with
your feelings and fully release them before you move on.

Time may ease the pain of loss, but being fully present with your
heartache brings healing. Be kind and gentle with yourself, and
transform your pain into a positive, creative force for a higher
good. When you emerge on the other side, you will see how
much stronger and lighter you are for all you have experienced.

I give myself the sacred space to
feel and heal the pain of loss.

THE DIVINE HAS YOUR BACK

"Opening our heart in gratitude brings us into grace."

– DR. DEBRA REBLE

Letting go into the unknown can be scary. You may waver between wanting change and fearing what the unknown will bring. It's easy to let go when you have a map right in front of you; yet, it can be difficult, even paralyzing, to let go of a relationship, a job, or life as you have known it.

That is when you need to trust that the divine has your back as well as your heart. Trust this connection to your spiritual source, let go, and allow the divine unfolding of your life. Letting go is about the completion of life cycles and thus, signals a beginning more than an end.

I choose to let go into trust.

SOUL TO SOUL

"I give love unconditionally, and it flows into my life."
– MARIANNE WILLIAMSON

Flowing in love defines a soul-hearted relationship, in which two or more individuals are connected heart to heart and soul to soul. Through this connection, people share an alchemy of love energy. When each person expresses their highest soul potential, contributing to the power of this stream, love flows unimpeded.

This flow of love sources from within each person and expands through offering it to another. The only way to sustain the flow of love is to give it away. When you give love without expecting love in return, unconditional love can flow freely in your life.

I give love unconditionally,
and it flows into my life.

LOVING YOURSELF FULLY

"Live with true intention and discover the part of you that loves to sing, dance, laugh, love, live, and embrace the magic inside!"

– ELAINE GIBSON

Being happy with yourself, even when you're alone, is the basis for being truly happy in a relationship. Before you can fully enter into a healthy partnership with another, you need to develop an intimate partnership with yourself.

Visualize yourself walking through your life happy, joyful, and fully alive. Write down this vision of your life as you see it now, as you imagine it will be in six months, and how you would like it to be in five years. Then choose three steps you can take toward manifesting your vision today—and act on them.

I choose to be happy in full partnership with myself.

WITNESS THE TRUTH OF OTHERS

"We are soul-wired to love and be loved."

– DR. DEBRA REBLE

Listen open-heartedly to another person's truth without judgment or criticism. Simply witness it. You need not, and cannot, always agree with them. As much as you may try to walk in another's shoes, see what they see, or feel what they feel, you can never have their experience.

Honor the experience of another person without trying to change it. Trust that they are following their own spiritual path, no matter what it may look like at the time. Accept that they are co-creating the life situations they need for their own growth, in the way that is best aligned with their soul's path.

I accept and honor the
spiritual path of others.

EMBRACE YOUR IMPERFECTION

*"I've often found that the more I pretend to be brave,
the braver I actually become."*

– SUSAN WILKING HORAN

Step out of the shadows of shame, stop beating yourself up,
and forgive your past choices. Wearing this cloak of shame only
makes you invisible by silencing your voice, squelching your spirit,
and suppressing your full self-expression. It keeps you from fully
opening to the divine essence of who you are.

Before you can heal and fully love yourself, you need to embrace
those messy, imperfect parts of you. To release your shame and
realize you are worthy of love, you must reveal who you truly are.

I love all of me, even the messy,
imperfect parts.

EMBRACE YOUR INNER CHILD

*"When you find joy in everything you do, you
will be living your highest purpose."*

– YAELLE SCHWARCZ

Discover your capacity to play and connect with your inner
child. When you do, laughter comes easily, as does the ease and
flexibility in playing with all possibilities in life. Invent or seek out
new activities that allow you to play with joyful abandon, such as
dancing in the rain or singing your heart out.

Infuse your life with humor, silliness, and play. Experience the
wonder of life as you did when you were a child. Let your life
evolve miraculously by embracing the philosophy of "Let's see
what's next."

I play with all the possibilities
that life has to offer.

SPIRITUAL RESILIENCE

*"Compassion helps us step out of our feelings of
separation and disconnection and into the shared
human experience, where love can flourish."*

– LISA HINTON

Your spiritual resilience makes it possible not only to endure
challenging situations but to use the information gleaned from
them for your spiritual growth. Your spirit is stronger than any
challenge you can ever face. Knowing you are resilient, you can
transcend any experience, even the most devastating event, and
rise up to face it.

There is a spiritual lining to every challenge in your life. Whether
or not you see it is the difference between it being a miracle or a
mess. Choose to see the miracle.

My spirit is stronger than any
challenging situation I can face.

TRUST BEYOND FEAR

"Wielding our power as beings of love helps us reach
our fullest soul potential and inspires others to reach theirs,
thereby making the world a better place."

– DR. DEBRA REBLE

Trust that there is a spiritual purpose to the chain of events that happen in your life even when they seem like random coincidences. Such events that lead to making your dreams a reality may appear random; yet, they reflect divine synchronicity. These divinely timed happenings show you that the universe is conspiring with you.

Divine timing occurs when you trust beyond fear, declare your intentions, and allow the universe to co-create with you on an elevated timetable. During such synchronistic experiences, you receive spiritual information that guides you toward manifesting your intentions. Trust your heart, and you will know what your next choice is and when to implement it.

When I trust divine timing,
I manifest my dreams beyond
what I can imagine.

RELEASING CO-DEPENDENCY

*"There's only one thing you've ever had to do to deserve
all that you want in this life: you were born."*

– GENEVIEVE KOHN

Your co-dependent patterns can attract you to unhealthy
relationships, emotional crutches to avoid your feelings of
insecurity. Looking for love and security outside yourself may
temporarily distract you from your feelings of lovelessness. Yet,
these unhealthy relationships woven of co-dependent patterns
can keep you from developing a whole and healthy relationship
with yourself.

Let go of any co-dependent relationships that weigh heavily on
you. Change your patterns of overhelping, over-cooperating, and
being overly responsible in your relationships. This will not only
empower you but also your relationships.

I release my co-dependent
patterns in relationships.

ANXIETY AS A SPIRITUAL GIFT

*"The changes you seek, hide behind habits and keep
you from making the shift."*

– CRYSTAL COCKERHAM

The power of awareness gives you the ability to shift your anxiety and see the spiritual information that is there to guide you. Once you are aware of your anxiety and call it out into the open, you have the power to diffuse and release it.

Ask your heart, "Is this an anxiety or fear that I've felt before?" If the answer is yes, this is the past coming up to claim the present. You don't need to force a new response just let this moment of self-awareness sink in. Be gentle with yourself and remain in your heart space. If you find yourself reacting out of fear, take a few deep breaths, and sit with this feeling until it passes.

I am aware of the spiritual
information that my anxiety
is showing me.

UPROOT UNHEALTHY PATTERNS

*"Everything begins with how you see and think
about yourself. Manifesting starts from within, and works
its way out into your reality."*

– MAL DUANE CPC, CRC

Experiencing your vulnerability is the catalyst for much needed physical, emotional, and spiritual healing. Like Humpty Dumpty falling off the wall, you may feel as if you are shattering into a million pieces. With this release, only your insecurities have died, and you can experience what it feels like to be fully alive.

Face your deepest insecurities and allow yourself to uproot unhealthy patterns and behaviors. Know that the stronger your reaction, the more deeply seated your vulnerability is to that pattern, person, or situation. Once you become aware of the source of your vulnerability, you can unblock your energies, freeing you to create what you truly want in your life.

I embrace my vulnerability as a
catalyst for personal transformation.

WHOLEHEARTED TRUST

*"You choose how you perceive, define, and respond
to your life. Transformation begins the moment you
start changing what you believe."*

– KATT TOZIER

Let go of what others think about your choices and trust
yourself wholeheartedly. Sometimes decisions can make some
of your closest friends and family panic, or even question your
sanity. Yet, their reactions allow you to see how afraid people
can become when they're challenged to look at themselves and
their own choices.

Follow your heart, even if it means standing up to people you
love or powerful authority figures. Have the confidence to trust
yourself and make soul-hearted choices that align with your heart.

I trust myself, let go of what others
think, and make the decisions that
align with my heart.

SACRED SOLITUDE

*"Special joy can be found in sharing our talents and gifts.
Knowing we brighten others' lives brings blessings to our own,
so be blessed. Let's share!"*

– MARGARET-MAGGIE HONNOLD

Solitude is good for the soul. A balanced and peaceful life begins with taking time to go within and radiates out to all aspects of your life. It's essential to create sacred space to be alone even if you are in a relationship. Such introspection opens opportunities for self-discovery, self-reflection, and connects you to your divine source.

Spend time alone to get to know and love yourself. Create a safe sanctuary to discover what makes you feel deeply and passionately. Taking time alone sustains your connection with your heart, your true being, and your soul's journey.

I choose time alone to be in touch
with my true being.

CONSCIOUS CHOICES

*"Forgiveness frees us from the past and opens an
energetic space for us to create a better future."*

– DR. DEBRA REBLE

At this time in your spiritual evolution, you are called to examine
your life, become aware of how you use your energies, and make
inspired choices that resonate with your soul's path. You have the
ability to consciously co-create your reality instead of giving away
your power to others or your circumstances.

When you operate as the source of love, you make choices
that are not bound by the limits of race, gender, culture, or the
dictates of others. You live more authentically and can choose in
accordance what's best for you and the inhabitants of the earth.

I make conscious choices from my
heart that serve my highest and
greatest good.

CHOOSE LOVE OVER FEAR

"Living your purpose isn't something that you necessarily aim to do. It is the natural result of a life lived in consult with your inner voice."

– FELICIA BAUCOM

All relationships are opportunities to open and connect at the heart level. In every moment, you demonstrate fear or love. The more you express love toward others, the more you see that you are lovable, and discover how to love more intimately.

Being lovingly connected with someone can bring out the best in you, and allow you to emotionally and spiritually grow. The relationship can become a catalyst to your own and the other person's transformation.

I invite in love and connection at the soul level.

LOVING ACKNOWLEDGMENT

*"Your heart is like a rosebud opening each petal until
the rose is in full bloom, releasing your unique
fragrance of love."*

– ANNA-CHARLOTTE HANDLER

Bless and release a relationship with love, gratitude, and integrity.
Take responsibility for co-creating the relationship as well as
letting it go. Lovingly acknowledge the purpose the relationship
has served in your life and the ways in which you have spiritually
grown from it. This practice empowers you to spiritually progress
and create space for new fulfilling relationships in the future.

I bless and release any relationship
with love and gratitude.

A NEW DAY IS HERE

*"You're not alone on this journey - take advantage of
your divine tools and claim your birthright - your most abundant,
fulfilling, and rewarding life."*

– JAMI HEARN

View sunrise as a time for opening to fresh possibilities and
new beginnings. What happened yesterday is wiped clean, and
you begin anew. Be grateful for another day, an opportunity to
spiritually grow, and a chance to live your best life. As the sun
dips below the horizon, let it be a time for releasing any unwanted
energies or disappointments.

Observe nature's cycles and note the parallels in your own life
and how your physical existence is based on such cycles. Create
personal rituals based on the seasons, the cycles of the moon,
or the cycle of each day. Notice how they afford you a spiritual
clarity that promotes healing and a sense of wholeness.

I am grateful for the cyclical
transformations of life and the
healing they provide me.

A CONDUIT OF LOVE

"By blessing the space with our divine presence, we radiate love to others and our world."

– DR. DEBRA REBLE

By loving yourself wholeheartedly, you can change the world. You become a conduit for love energy when you fully embrace and express your true nature—which is, and has always been, love. The more you love yourself, the more you connect compassionately with others and become an ambassador of love in the world.

Loving yourself creates an energetic ripple that radiates outward from your heart center and shifts everything in its path. When you emanate the high vibration of love, you not only receive the benefits but also raise the vibration of those around you.

When I love myself, I create a ripple of love out into the world.

DAILY SELF-CARE

*"Our purpose is not to survive our life but to live it
to the full and radiate out our brightness
to support others on their way."*

– TONIA BROWNE

Restorative self-care is composed of simple and sacred acts of kindness toward yourself. Give yourself self-care by engaging in simple daily rituals such as taking a few minutes for yourself at the beginning and end of the day to meditate, journal, or just be. Transform your daily shower or bath into a clearing ritual to cleanse your energy field after a stressful day.

Engage in activities such as walking, yoga, massage, acupuncture, or energy work to release tension or toxicity, opening you to the flow of positive energy. Make a commitment to practice one act of restorative self-care every day. Entering into this covenant with yourself will sustain your happiness and well-being.

I commit to practicing one act
of self-care every day.

AN ELEVATED PERSPECTIVE

"The heart is the Divine Messenger of the soul.
Your truth beats deep within your inner knowing seeking
the rhythm that allows your spirit to sing."

– JOANNE LUSSIER

Transcend any challenging situation by imagining yourself flying
in a plane and looking down at the ground below. Viewing any
situation from a broader more spiritual perspective helps you
perceive it as an opportunity for healing and spiritual growth.
Your point of view from spirit takes in the situation from three
hundred and sixty degrees.

As such, you can move outside of whatever is happening in your
life so you can transcend any situation with healthy detachment.
Every experience you have, no matter how challenging, can then
be viewed through this spiritual lens as an opportunity to grow.

I view all situations from an elevated
perspective, seeing the opportunity
to spiritually grow.

THE DIVINE ESSENCE OF LOVE

"You take your life in your own hands, and what happens?
A terrible thing, no one to blame."

– ERICA JONG

Embracing your deepest vulnerabilities is the path to healing yourself. You may be afraid that if you let your guard down, let someone in, or let yourself be seen, you won't be good enough. Yet, when you lean into your insecurities and vulnerabilities, you are more open to transformation. It's in these dark moments of the soul that you peel away the hard shell of your protective patterns, and reveal the light of your being.

Release the negative messages that tell you that you are not good enough, lovable enough, or worthy enough. Listen to the gentle, loving voice of your heart that reminds you that you are more than enough, no matter what you do or don't do, because you are the essence of love.

I am more than enough because
I am the divine essence of love.

PRESENCE AS A GIFT OF LOVE

"Our minds fill in blanks to craft a whole story. Unfortunately, what we make up is often wrong. Remain curious and ask questions instead of creating false narratives."

– DEBORAH KEVIN

Express love through your divine presence. When you are truly present with another person, not distracted or guarded, you open a portal of loving energy that facilitates intimate connection. Being present is having a conscious awareness of what's happening moment to moment without getting caught up in your own thoughts.

Looking deeply into another person's eyes, giving them your undivided attention, and listening with an open heart are all elements of being present. Your divine presence, more than any other aspect of love, shows that you are fully there for someone. It is in this sacred space that intimacy unfolds.

When I am fully present, I move through my daily life as a meditation.

THE POWER OF THE PAUSE

"Courage sources deep within our hearts as self-love, acceptance, and compassion."

– DR. DEBRA REBLE

Give yourself the "permission to pause" in any situation that triggers a negative reaction. Take the time to step back and observe the situation from a more expansive perspective. After pushing the pause button, take a few deep breaths, open your heart, and release your reaction.

Taking such a purposeful pause brings awareness to the emotional root of your reaction and any self-destructive patterns it may have triggered. Sit with your reaction and allow your feelings to release, and then reflect on the spiritual information it is showing you.

I give myself permission to pause, reflect, and release any negative reaction.

TRUST IN DIVINE ORDER

*"Hold the high vibration of your vision with every inspired
action to accelerate change and move towards your dream life
faster than you ever believed."*

– ANN SANFELIPPO

Acknowledge the divine order that exists in everything around you and within you. Align yourself with this natural flow, release your perceived control, and move effortlessly through your daily experiences.

Notice that your feelings of tension ease and you can fully engage in each moment with a deeper level of enjoyment. As you release your need for control and align with the flow of energy of the universe, you move through your life with ease and grace.

When I align with the flow of divine energy, I move through my day with ease and grace.

HEALTHY CAREGIVING

*"When we shine a light on what is already going well,
we illuminate the path."*

– EMILY MADILL

Healthy caregiving is a loving, energetic exchange in which
you are the channel for light energy. This exchange results in a
positive energy flow through the heart center first to yourself
and then to others. However, the pattern of caretaking can take
its toll on you physically, emotionally, and spiritually. "Taking
care" instead of "giving care" can lead to energetic depletion and
physical and emotional vulnerability.

As a true caregiver, open your heart compassionately in healthy
detachment and maintain a positive flow of energy with the
other person without suffering or absorbing their energies.
Compassionate detachment keeps you from taking things to
heart, thereby, preventing compassion fatigue.

I give care instead of taking care.

EMBODY LOVE AND LIGHT

*"Do you really want to look back on your life and
see how wonderful it could have been had you not
been afraid to live it?"*

– CAROLINE MYSS

Whether you are going abroad or down the street, travel as
an ambassador of love. Step outside of your familiar habits,
cultural comfort zones, and expand your horizons. Let go of any
expected outcomes and welcome the enhanced love, joy, and play
that streams into your life. Travel can transport you beyond old
patterns, open your imagination, and inspire new experiences.

Leave any space that you move through better by your kind
actions and positive energies. Choose to love unconditionally
and radiate beams of love each step along the way. All it takes is
present awareness and the willingness to be the embodiment of
love and light.

I travel through my life as a love
ambassador, sharing light and love
wherever I go.

DROP INTO YOUR HEART SPACE

*"Turn your life experience into your passion
career to find joy, blessings, and your life purpose.
You'll transform your life and others."*

– CORNELIA WARD

Just dropping into your heart space can create calm and balance
in your nervous system. Focus your attention to your heart to
bring your body, mind, and spirit into energetic balance. Put your
hand on your heart and take a deep breath to signal to your body
to drop into your heart space, breathe deeply, and relax.

You can also use a visual cue such as a stop sign or pause button
to prevent any fear or anxiety from escalating whenever you are
triggered. Visualize this cue, or place it on or near a phone or
desk, where situations may arise that provoke anxiety. Let it be
an automatic reminder to pause, release your anxiety, and then
consciously respond.

I can take a deep breath
and drop into my heart space
to release my anxiety.

ABUNDANCE FLOWS

"Your inner unrest is your Soul whispering to you,
'Remember me. Hear Me. Allow me to lead you.'"

– LINDA JOY

Abundance flows freely into your life when you let go of any expectations or conditions. You may think you can create abundance by forcing it to happen through sheer will. Even though your intention may be good, this mindset blocks the flow of energy due to your focus being on the outcome rather than on giving with no strings attached.

Give a gift, pay a bill, or offer assistance to someone without any restrictions. Then receive acts of kindness, compliments, or gifts graciously. When you give and receive beyond any expectation, the harmonious balance of energy in your life is naturally restored.

Abundance flows into my life
when I give without any expectations
or conditions.

SPEAK YOUR TRUTH

*"The middle ground, between dreams and reality, is where
my path unfurls before me, where I emerge in my truth
and let my light shine. Possibility in action!"*

– KRIS GROTH

Being heard means being acknowledged for who you are.
Sometimes you may feel misunderstood, disconnected, or not
heard. You may doubt whether your experience is valid or
worthwhile when it differs from another person's. All the more
reason to speak your truth from your heart.

Speak your truth from your heart and express yourself openly and
honestly. When you speak from this clear and powerful source,
love permeates your words, making them easier to be received and
accepted. Genuine and loving words open a person's listening to
you, and your words take on a greater, more heartfelt meaning.

When I speak my truth from my
heart, I am heard for who I am.

ENERGETIC BOUNDARIES

"The act of conversing with the part of you who is overwhelmed by fears, as you would with any scared child, can be invaluable in your healing journey."

– MICHELLE DEEB

Establishing healthy energetic boundaries is key to producing a positive flow of energy in your relationships. All relationships are energetic exchanges between people. When healthy boundaries are in place, the flow of energy is growth-promoting, for you and the other person. Without such boundaries in place, you can easily exhaust your energy by absorbing the unwanted energies of others.

Create healthy energetic boundaries by opening your heart compassionately in healthy detachment without taking on the other person's energies. Such detachment keeps you from taking things to heart, which can stress your heart center, resulting in physical and emotional distress or depression.

I establish healthy energetic boundaries for my well-being and well-being of my relationships.

LET YOUR LIGHT SHINE

*"Embrace your Becoming. Like a seed buried in the darkness,
your soul's purpose is drawn toward the light so it can
blossom into beauty."*

– JOANNE LUSSIER

A world of love begins with you. You can influence the lives
of others and elevate the consciousness in the world by raising
your vibration to love. You can take responsibility for the energy
you project into the world by becoming more conscious of your
thoughts, feelings, and choices.

Open your heart and let your light shine out into the world. Join
your light with others to bring about a greater good, peace, and
love to all human beings. It is this universal force that will bring
about the evolution of human consciousness to love.

Through elevating my vibration
to love, I let my light shine out
into the world.

PRACTICE LOVING KINDNESS

"As we become more present to our patterns,
they began to loosen their grip ... and we expand into
a more vast and deep version of ourselves."

– DR. CATHERINE HAYES, CPCC

You are the source of the inner and outer landscape of your life.
You can complain about how difficult life is, or you can bless
the people and situations that help you spiritually grow. Let a
challenging situation just be until you can respond with patience,
non-reactivity, and tolerance.

You can say "bless and release" to shift the energy on any
negative situation. Practice loving kindness, non-judgment,
and forgive quickly and often. Open your heart, offer support,
and express love fully, passionately and beyond conditions.

I allow a situation to just be so I can
respond with patience and tolerance.

IN THE SPACE OF CREATION

"To lovingly connect, we must reveal who we truly are."

– DR. DEBRA REBLE

Hold steady, open your heart, and trust yourself no matter what is happening in your life. Keep in mind that you are preparing for your future and are being given an amazing opportunity to change direction, clear your path of anything that doesn't serve you, and set new intentions of what truly does.

Love yourself and let go of more in your life than ever before. By letting go of what you no longer need or want, you are opening to a myriad of new possibilities. This is the space of creation and is positive, no matter what it looks like at the time.

I am open to the space of creation
and set my intentions.

LIVE WITH PASSION & PURPOSE

*"When you feel a sense of peace in your life, allow yourself
to completely bathe at that moment, feeling it with
all of your senses. Carry it with you."*

– JESSICA DUGAS

Live with passion and purpose by following your heart. Lead with your heart and shine the light of your beautiful being. When you live wholeheartedly, you will feel a sense of ease, trust, and alignment with your higher spiritual calling

You may be accustomed to "doing" more than "being." However, your true being is not the job you do, the roles you play, or how successful you are. It's embodying love, exuding joy, and making purposeful choices. This means being on purpose in every moment no matter what you are doing, where you are, or whom you are with.

I live with passion and purpose,
which fulfills my highest
spiritual calling.

THE ROAD LESS TRAVELED

*"Money is always flowing somewhere, even during a recession.
If you develop a mindset that allows you to seek it out,
you'll do exceptionally well."*

– LORENE COLLIER

The path of transformation is the road less traveled. When there has been, or you anticipate, a major change in your life, old patterns may be triggered. They can also arise during a transition or when you are about to realize a dream. This happens because of your increased vulnerability during times of transformation.

Transformation calls for clearing your life of any patterns that hold you back from fulfilling your soul's potential. Trust that you are prepared for any change in your life or you wouldn't be going through it.

I am prepared to clear my life of
any patterns that impede the
realization of my dreams.

MAKE YOUR HEART SING

"In a world of cookie cutter formulas, a real voice can make a real big difference. Let old words go and see life grow!"

– KATHLEEN GUBITOSI, MA

Give yourself permission to "just be" and let go of your preconceived beliefs of how you should live. Choose to follow your heart.

As a child, you yielded to this freedom of spirit knowing that nothing else really mattered. However, as an adult, you may feel resigned, overwhelmed, and even tired from the challenging pace of endless to-do lists that require your time and attention.

Give yourself time to just be. Spend time playing, having fun, and taking pleasure in the simple things in life. Do what makes your heart sing, and your true being comes alive.

I give myself permission to just be.

SURRENDER OLD HABITS

*"The universe holds all the things we need in our lives.
The problem is society expects it to be handed to them.
You have to ask for it to receive."*

– CERI RIDENOUR

With any new beginning, surrender old habits, belief systems, and patterns that no longer serve your highest self. You may feel as if the grids beneath your feet are shifting and your internal landscape is being altered. It's all in preparation for you to step up and fulfill your soul's potential. The universe has amped up the vibration so you can be clear of your soul's purpose and live it.

Hold this stretch between your spirit and body or "heaven and earth," by grounding yourself, paying attention to spiritual signs, and choosing consciously. Integrate the information you receive by taking the time to go within and listen to your heart.

I surrender all that no longer
serves me, so I am clear of my
soul's path and purpose.

WHISPER OF SPIRIT

*"Fear enables me to go deeper into myself to release
and heal old baggage. Each time my soul's windows get clearer,
allowing my light to shine brighter."*

– KRIS GROTH

Tune into the whisper of spirit through your heart instead of listening to the negative beliefs of your head. You can learn to distinguish between the thoughts that have run your life in the past and the new possibilities emerging through your heart.

Listening to your inner wisdom helps you develop a more conscious relationship with yourself. You have sensitivities that guide your life whether it is a gut feeling, an "aha" moment, or an inner knowing. When you are inspired or "in-spirited," you open to this flow of information and invite spirit to guide you to make better choices in your life.

I tune in to the whisper of spirit
through my heart.

YOUR DIVINE SUPPORT TEAM

"If we want to teach our children that they are worthy and lovable—we have to embrace our own self-love and worthiness."

– DR. DEBRA REBLE

Observe your relationships to see who serves a supportive role in your life. Many support systems are set up to perpetuate the patterns of struggle, failure, victimization, or even illness. Instead, select a healthy energetic support system comprised of psychotherapists, spiritual guides, or soul-connected friends who encourage your spiritual transformation.

Let go of being supported in any way that is conditional, even by family and friends, and establish a soul team that guides you unconditionally. Surround yourself with people that positively support your well-being and assist in your spiritual progression.

I surround myself with people who love and support me unconditionally.

THE GIFT OF FORGIVENESS

*"Passion is energy. Feel the power that comes
from focusing on what excites you."*

– OPRAH

Forgive yourself quickly and often for not being perfect or
having a perfect life. Open your heart in compassion and forgive
yourself for the imperfect choices that have brought you here to
this perfect moment.

The greatest gift you can give yourself is forgiveness. It
transmutes judgment into acceptance and makes the past
powerless over you. Find the courage to forgive yourself, the
strength to suspend shame, and the self-compassion to release
your suffering. This creates new space in your heart for you to
love yourself.

I forgive myself and my past choices
with loving compassion.

WHOLE AND COMPLETE

"There is a magnificent source of energy that runs, breathes, and lives within you. Live your life, day by day, from the perspective of your divinity."

– LILIANA VANASCO

Being in a relationship with another person requires you to first open your heart and love yourself unconditionally. When you love yourself, you become your own safe haven, where you feel free to fully express love and who you are.

Opening your heart and loving yourself without qualification is the foundation for developing a healthy, committed, and loving relationship. Be mindful that you are whole and complete just as you are.

I am whole and complete in myself, and I offer this to others.

ACCEPTANCE

*"Without passion turning the light on, no one
will ever see the glow. You might not use what you know
right away, but never let knowledge go to waste."*

– LORENE COLLIER

Accept any situation no matter how uncomfortable, difficult, or painful as an opportunity for personal transformation. Like a surfer riding a huge wave, it takes awareness, balance, and flexibility to keep from falling off your board and being caught in the undertow of life.

Instead of reacting from fear, anger, or resistance, respond with conscious awareness and trust that what is happening is for your greater good. See it as an opportunity to release what doesn't work in your life and take a different approach.

I accept any situation as a spiritual opportunity to transform my life.

A COMPASSIONATE HEART

"Like a pebble dropped into a pond, our intention sets off an energetic vibration that radiates outward from our heart centers and shifts everything in our path."

– DR. DEBRA REBLE

Visualize any person you need to forgive as a spiritual being. Seeing them in this light makes it easier to forgive them and their human frailties. Bless their spirit in white light. Then, release their dysfunctional patterns and poor choices in pink light. The vibration of pink light governs the physical universe and short-circuits negativity, thereby isolating it.

The more you open your heart in compassion and forgive them, the more you eliminate negative energy. This creates new space for positive energy to return to you.

I open my heart in forgiveness by
seeing the light of all beings.

FOCUS ON YOURSELF

"Remind yourself every day that you are allowed to be happy and unlimited in every aspect of your life."

– KELLY MISHELL

Whenever people come into your life, they often show you something about yourself that you need to release or transform. Be mindful that you have the ability to pause, the power to disengage, and the knowledge of who you truly are.

Take the focus off the difficult person and place it on yourself. Use this as an opportunity to illuminate and shift the situation from the inside out. If you change yourself in response to any person, then the relationship will change.

I can change any relationship
when I change myself.

A POSITIVE OUTLOOK

*"Every thought, word, and action you put forth is
an energetic memo to the universe."*

– DR. DEBRA REBLE

When you hold a positive outlook on life, you are more likely to
manage life's challenges better. It also helps you live longer, supports
a healthy immune system, and sustains a sense of happiness.

Appreciate the positive experiences in your life by bringing your
full attention to the present moment. Dwelling on the positive
aspects of your life is the essence of moving toward the tipping
point of positivity. This allows for genuine resilience in your
mind, body, and spirit.

I keep a positive outlook on life,
which makes me resilient to any
stress in my life.

TRANSITIONAL PAUSES

*"I have learned from my dogs that there is enough
joy in the present moment that you can overcome
any and all pain from past events."*

– ANN MARIE HOFF

Your spiritual progression ebbs and flows with periods of intense forward movement, which gives way to periods of transitional pauses.

In these moments, you may feel discouraged; however, you don't ever really go backward. You may pause momentarily because there is a new obstacle in your path or a new layer of an old pattern to clear, but the spiritual work you have done cannot be undone.

Every step on your spiritual path is meaningful. Sometimes an intense growth spurt requires that you rest for a period of time to fully integrate the new positive energies that have awakened and are becoming available to you.

I trust every step on my spiritual path
moves me forward in some way.

CHERISH YOURSELF

"Being playful naturally liberates the mind, opens the heart,
and lifts the spirit. Take time to play today."

– DR. DEBRA REBLE

Cultivate self-compassion by accepting all aspects of yourself
without reservation. Eliminate all of the violent thoughts, words,
and actions you inflict upon yourself. Stop beating yourself up
or putting yourself down every time you see an imperfection or
make a mistake.

Instead, realize that all of your thoughts, feelings, and choices
originate in your being as love. Nurture yourself with all the
kindness and compassion you would shower on someone you
cherish. With this comes a sense of love, inner peace, and
spiritual attunement with everyone and everything.

I practice loving-kindness and
compassion toward myself.

YOUR DIVINE SAFETY NET

"The greatest act of courage is to be and to own all of who you are — without apology, without excuses, without masks to cover the truth of who you are."

– DEBBIE FORD

Trusting yourself takes more than deep breaths and positive mantras. It requires a conscious connection to your divine source. Like having a safety net while walking on a high wire, absolute trust in yourself is your safety net.

Sometimes you may feel like you are operating in your life without a secure lifeline. Yet, your connection to divine source is your inner security, your divine safety net. You are not alone as your divine source is always with you.

Trusting yourself governs how you respond to the challenges in your life. It gives you the personal power to express love, flow with the stream of life, and transcend even the most difficult circumstances.

I trust my connection with the divine source as my inner security.

RELEASE SELF-LOVE BLOCKS

"Playful interludes, which focus on BEING rather than DOING, help us restore balance and deepen intimacy."

– DR. DEBRA REBLE

Releasing energy blocks opens you to self-love. Like removing the kinks from a garden hose to open the flow of water, you need to release anything that impedes the flow of your energy. When you harbor resentment, you block the flow of energy in your body and become more prone to dis-ease.

Sit quietly and scan your body beginning with your feet, moving up through the top of your head. Notice where you are holding tension, tightness, or pain. Put your attention there and breathe love energy into this space.

Ask yourself, "What am I holding onto? What is the origin of this pain? What am I being guided to see and release?" Journal your responses.

When I release energy blocks in my body, I open the flow of love and restore balance.

GUIDANCE OF YOUR SPIRIT

"No matter how difficult and painful it may be, nothing sounds as good to the soul as the truth."

– MARTHA BECK

Tuning into the inner guidance of your spirit helps you develop a more conscious relationship with your true being. When you open your heart, you invite spirit to guide you. Its whisper provides a flow of spiritual information you can use to make better, more inspired choices in your life.

The voice of your spirit reminds you of who you are and what your heart most desires. Open your heart and tune into the guidance of your spirit. It will lead to a richer, more expansive way of living—even when it takes you down a more challenging path.

I open my heart to the
guidance of my spirit.

DIVINE GRACE IN MOTION

*"By bringing greater awareness and presence
to our personality structures, we can release these masks
and wake up to our true self."*

– DR. CATHERINE HAYES, CPCC

When you walk in beauty, you are divine grace in motion.
Your feminine energy is a source of strength, compassion,
and courage. What makes you strong, loving, and confident is
embracing your vulnerability, listening to your inner wisdom,
and calling upon your feminine power whenever you need it.

Embody your divine feminine and express this powerful energy
in your life. Through your feminine spirit, make love with life,
play with passion, and live with purpose in every moment.

I embrace my divine feminine power
and express this energy in the world.

SHIFT YOUR PERSPECTIVE

*"One of the most empowering awakenings we can have
is to listen to the wisdom of our intuition and then—in all
trust have the courage to follow it."*

– LIZETE MORAIS

When you lead with your heart, you create a harmonious flow of energy in your life. Integrating your head and heart elevates you to a higher level of awareness. For example, when you swim, you tend to focus on your strokes. Once you let go of your mind and shift your focus to your heart, you begin to move meditatively through the water without thinking.

Shift your perspective from the eyes in your head to the eyes of your heart. Tune into what you sense, feel, or intuit and let this information guide you on your soul's path. BE light of heart and see who you are and who you came here to BE.

I view my life through the
eyes of my heart.

THE BEAUTY OF YOUR BEING

"Being present is living daily life as meditation."

– DR. DEBRA REBLE

When you cultivate compassion for yourself by being kind, nonjudgmental, and nonreactive, you are more likely to act this way toward others. Such action generates love and inner peace. When you are truly compassionate with yourself, you never stop seeing the beauty of your being as love.

Live as a compassionate being. Trust that every human being is on their own spiritual path. This increases your capacity to create peace and harmony in your life because it reminds you of the interconnectedness of all life.

I live in compassion, which connects
me with myself and others
in divine love.

SOUL-WIRED BONDS

*"Awaken each day and think only about today,
not tomorrow. Live in the present."*

– DEBBIE SAIN-BISSETTE

Happy, healthy, and loving relationships are founded in physical, emotional, and spiritual connections. You have entered an "age of love" where love and connection have now become the foundation on which you commit to and create a relationship.

You are soul-wired to bond because you need love and connection not only to survive but to thrive. Love and connection help you deal with life's stressors and support your spiritual growth.

I create relationships grounded
love and connection.

STAYING GROUNDED

"You must trust that love has the power to open your heart, raise your vibration, and dissolve negativity."

– DR. DEBRA REBLE

One way to calm anxiety is by grounding your energies. Start by directing your attention into your feet. When you experience anxiety, your energy is mostly at the top of your head, which can make you feel detached from the rest of your body. This sudden rush of energy to your headspace may lead to feeling unsteady, dizzy, or even faint.

Focus on how your feet feel inside your socks or shoes and against the ground. Once you have focused your attention here, tap your feet on the ground until you feel the energy. Doing this outside on grass or moss enhances the calming effect.

I ground my energies whenever I feel stressed, anxious, or in transition.

IMPECCABLE WITH YOUR WORD

"May whatever suffering arises serve to awaken compassion for yourself and the sacredness of healing for all beings."

– CINDY HIVELY

It's not always easy staying true to yourself and your word. However, your word is one of the most powerful forces of intention you have. When you are impeccable with your word, you see yourself and are seen by others as trustworthy.

The path of impeccability builds integrity. Your words reflect who you are and when you keep your word, you are seen by others as trustworthy. Be sincere and channel the power of your words by living a life of honesty and transparency.

I am impeccable with my word.

THE GPS OF YOUR SOUL

"Sunshine is a reflection of your inner light."

– TARAH ABRAM

Your heart is the GPS of your soul. It senses and transmits divine energy, bypassing the brain so you can receive spiritual information. Every person is born with the ability to be an open channel of spiritual information, for it is their divine nature.

Although you may tune in to this energy differently, you tap into the same divine energy. How open you are and how much you trust yourself determines the extent you can channel this energy. It may be natural and easy for you; for others, it may take continuous practice. Yet, channeling this divine source of energy creates a fulfilling and purposeful life and sustains all that is well and good.

I am an open channel of
spiritual information.

VIBRATIONAL ALIGNMENT

"Forgiveness frees us from the past and opens an energetic space for us to create a better future."

– DR. DEBRA REBLE

When you open your heart, you create coherence as your head aligns vibrationally with your heart rhythms. You may sense a tingling or warming sensation, goose bumps, or a subtle vibration in parts of your body. This experience may feel like a sunburst, with waves of warm energy radiating from the center of your chest outward into the world.

In such a state of open-heartedness, you feel relaxed, calm, and centered. You express gratitude and enjoy a sense of peace, harmony, and love. By opening your heart, you create this energetic coherence to prevent stress and enhance mental clarity.

I open my heart to reduce stress and create peace of mind.

A CHILD'S LOVE

"Transforming adversity with a loving flow of courage, wisdom, and resiliency, results in wondrous growth, development, and joy."

– BONNIE LARSON

Children love and connect in more open-hearted and unconditional ways than adults. They intuitively plug into to a field of divine energy that emanates from them. Through this connection to their divine source, they are continuously in touch with their infinite nature as love.

Immerse yourself in a child's love, joy, and imagination, and you will learn how to be uninhibited and playful again. Let a child reintroduce you to the wonders of stargazing, the glee of chasing butterflies, and the timelessness of a summer day. By being with them, you will commune with your heart and soul.

Through the energy of a child,
I commune with my heart and soul.

DECLARE YOUR INTENTIONS

"The blessing of letting go creates sacred space for healing."

– DR. DEBRA REBLE

By declaring your intentions and taking inspired action, you co-create your reality. Like dropping a pebble into a pond, your intention sets off an energetic vibration that shifts everything in its path. You manifest your intention through one inspired action at a time.

Notice the opportunities that align with your intention and choose well. If you declare that you want a healthy, loving relationship, then as opportunities arise, make the choices supporting that beloved someone showing up in your life.

Courageously declare your intentions,
and take inspired action
to manifest them.

MAKE LOVE WITH LIFE

"It's time to make extraordinary your new normal."

– ELAINE GIBSON

Make love in every moment through whatever the universe gives you. Making love opens you to the flow of grace. When you express the essence of your soul, you transcend from making love to being love.

Make love with life by choosing what aligns with your soul. Consciously choose your thoughts, words, and actions. Be patient, tolerant, and flexible when life gets challenging, or things don't go your way. Keep an open heart and a great sense of humor no matter what is happening at the time.

I make love with life by living in alignment with my soul's path.

WHERE LOVE IS PRESENT

*"If we want to teach our children that they
are worthy and lovable—we have to embrace
our own self-love and worthiness."*

– DR. DEBRA REBLE

Where love is present, there are always miracles. While you may be reluctant to apply the word miracle to yourself, this only diminishes your healing power. Positive messages enhance your healing ability while negative ones deplete it. The cells in your body react to positive energy by supporting your immune system.

Visualize and direct the energy of love from your heart to surround every cell in your body. Like a laser beam, use this high vibrational energy to promote healing. You have the innate power to heal yourself through the vibration of love.

I can heal myself through the power of love.

LEAN INTO THE TENDER PLACES

"Each act of self-nurturing is an act of self-love."

– KELLEY GRIMES, MSW

Embracing your vulnerabilities opens you to spiritual transformation, for one unlocks the door to the other. It's difficult to open your heart to self-love when you are clutching your hurts so tightly. The release of your vulnerable pain is key to your "un-covery" to love.

Living a soul-hearted life isn't about perfection, it's about vulnerability. Embracing your vulnerability moves you from fear to courage. When you lean into these tender places, you discover that love has been there all along.

I embrace my vulnerable pain and discover love in its place.

CLEAR YOUR FEAR

"Before you can heal—before you can fully love and connect to yourself—you must embrace those messy, imperfect, parts of you."

– DR. DEBRA REBLE

Transcend fear by allowing things to be without resisting or avoiding change. Clear your fear and let go of all you hold onto from the past. Anything from your past can create an energy block that interferes with your health and well-being.

When you no longer hold on to anything, you give yourself the freedom to follow your heart. Move through your day without trying to force anything to happen. Create positive intentions and trust your spirit to guide your choices.

I clear my fear by allowing
things to just be.

LETTING A RELATIONSHIP GO

*"Your life is happening now. Follow the joy
and show up for the moments you have."*

– FELICIA BAUCOM

Just as you move through the cycles of life, so do your
relationships. You have a primary soul purpose in life as do each
of your relationships. You experience a multitude of relationships
throughout your life that fulfill different needs and bring out
diverse aspects of yourself. Some of these relationships remain
forever, while others come and go over a lifetime.

Many of the relationships that dissolve are based on specific
conditions such as a need for sex, support, stability, or
companionship. While these relationships can nurture, heal, and
soothe you, they are transitional and last only for a short time.
Recognize when a relationship's life cycle is complete and let it go.

I recognize when a relationship's life
cycle is complete and let it go.

OPEN YOUR HEART

"Self-compassion is nurturing yourself with all the kindness and love you would shower on someone you cherish."

– DR. DEBRA REBLE

Opening your heart awakens you to your authentic self and your essence as love. Seeing yourself through the eyes of your heart, acknowledge that you are love and, therefore, more than enough. Knowing you are love dissolves fear, and your true being emerges. It shows you that you are a divine energy source capable of creating a fulfilling and purposeful life.

Spend five minutes a day before you get out of bed opening your heart and connecting to yourself. When you connect to yourself, you trust that you are the source of love.

I open my heart and know that
I am my own source of love.

TRUST THEIR JOURNEY

*"We do not need magic to change the world, we carry
all the power we need inside ourselves already: we have
the power to imagine better."*

– J.K. ROWLING

You cannot know another person's soul journey. You must trust
that whatever choices they make are part of their divine path. As
difficult as it is to understand, they are fulfilling their soul's plan
even if that choice is death.

Be grateful for the precious time you have had with them whether
it's a few seconds, months, or years. Regardless of the time you
spent together, your love and connection transcends the physical
universe and resides in the eternal space of the soul.

I am grateful for the love and
connection with another even if the
time is limited.

BE COURAGEOUS

"Do cartwheels. Find a reason to decorate a cake. Discover the parachute moment that makes you say, 'I live for this!'"

– SUSAN KAY DAHL

Be courageous and speak your truth honestly and openly with your whole heart. Share your thoughts without worrying about how other people will react. Being courageous doesn't mean performing acts of external strength, but boldly acting on and speaking your truth in the face of fear.

Speaking your truth is one of the most courageous choices you can make. Be courageous by loving and accepting yourself fully. Become your own hero, step into your power, not as a frightened human being, but as a powerful beacon of hope and courage.

I am courageous when I step into
my light and speak my truth.

SPIRITUAL COMPLETION

"When you shift your negative thoughts to positive ones, you shift the vibrational frequency of your energy field from fear to courage."

– DR. DEBRA REBLE

Although you may have released an old pattern, sometimes you can "slip" and find yourself caught up in the residue of it. Releasing the layers of patterns is a lifelong process because the pattern's energy never completely goes away. Instead, the layers become more subtle, and it takes more awareness to recognize them.

Even when you spiritually complete a pattern, the brain continues to show a hologram of it. Like a file that you have deleted from your hard drive, its virtual energy acts as a hologram that still can surface. It alerts you when the pattern shows up and reminds you to stay true to yourself.

When I slip into an old pattern, I'm being reminded to be true to myself.

APPRECIATE THE BLESSINGS

"Just as a seed grows with the warmth of the sun, so our positive qualities grow when we put our attention on them."

– ARIELLE FORD

Live in the graceful flow of gratitude. Wake up every morning with a sense of appreciation for what the universe has in store for you. Before your feet even touch the floor, open your heart and give thanks for the new day in front of you.

Close your eyes, place a hand on the center of your chest, and focus your attention on your heart. Radiate love in the form of gratitude to yourself and then to others. Accept life as it comes today, and be grateful for even the simplest things. Appreciate the blessings of who you are and what you already have in your life.

When I live in the flow of gratitude,
I open to grace.

WINDS OF CHANGE

"Look to the change of the seasons and nature for healing and inspiration."

– CHARLOTTE BIFULCO

Autumn is a time of transformation. It is a season of permanence and change where you find the inner reserve of strength to change as well. Take advantage of this time and go within. In the space of your inner being, you will know what needs to shift.

Use this regenerative time to reflect on what needs to change in your life. When faced with change, instead of resisting it, respond with trust. Harness this creative energy positively for change. Let the winds of change carry your intentions forward into your future.

I reflect on what needs to change in my life.

THE RIPPLE OF SELF-LOVE

"Trust that you can heal or transform your life by accepting what's right in front of you, even when it's difficult."

– DR. DEBRA REBLE

Taking precious self-care is not self-indulgent, but essential to enhancing your health, well-being, and relationships. It increases your energy, brings peace of mind, and restores balance in your life.

Taking precious care of yourself is an aspect of self-love, which then ripples out to others. Even setting aside just five minutes a day to nurture yourself can help you reduce stress, calm the nervous system, and feel renewed.

I take precious care of myself as
an act of self-love.

YOUR FEMININE POWER

*"Never apologize for being sensitive or emotional.
Let this be a sign that you've got a big heart and aren't
afraid to let others see it."*

– BRIGITTE NICOLE

This is a time of intense transformation and an awakening of your feminine energy. As a spiritual midwife, you are being called to assist other women in the natural opening of their divine essence and expressing this powerful energy on earth.

It's time for you to step up and show up in your feminine power by tapping into your intuitive nature, listening to your heart's wisdom, and trusting your power to heal yourself and the world through love. This is your birthright and soul calling.

I step into my feminine power and
express that energy into the world.

THE FLOW OF ABUNDANCE

*"Don't is the most wasted word in the English language.
Because for dogs, teenagers, and the Universe, the negative
cancels out: so it means DO!"*

– ANN MARIE HOFF

The exchange of loving energy creates a flow of abundance in your life. For you to love more, you need to allow more love in. For you to have more abundance, you need to let go of control and trust that, while like inevitably attracts like, it does so on its own divine timetable.

The important aspect of this exchange is sustaining the flow of positive energy, not the form it takes. Opening your heart creates a flow of abundance that stands alone, separate from any and all conditions. It is an energetic gift in and of itself which brings you blessings a million times over.

When I open to the exchange of love, I create a flow of abundance.

A SHIFT IN CONSCIOUSNESS

"As lightworkers, we have a special need to heal our wounded child so that we can initiate and facilitate the healing of others and our world."

– DR. DEBRA REBLE

Sometimes a crisis opens you to spiritual transformation. This offers you a great gift because when you embrace it, you initiate an "experiential death." This metaphorical death allows you to release the past and attach to nothing except your own being. This creates a shift in your consciousness, much like dying and leaving the physical body.

Such a shift in your consciousness can be frightening or disorienting. But what really dies is your ego, not your true self. When you let go of your past self-definitions, your true being rises from the ashes like the phoenix. Just as you know light through darkness, so can you know life through death.

I let go of past self-definitions and allow my sacred truth to shine through.

AN AMBASSADOR OF LOVE

*"Serendipity flows into my life effortlessly, when I
am devoted to allowing myself to play and create,
persistently and wholeheartedly."*

— DEB "GYPSYOWL" BRYAN

Be an ambassador of love. As a member of Team Love, you are here
to facilitate the world's evolution to universal love. Using your power
as love helps you reach your fullest soul potential and inspires others
to reach theirs, thereby making the world a better place.

When you interact with others, acknowledge them through eye
contact and a smile. Let people feel completely seen and heard
in your presence. Draw them into a loving space by softening
your gaze and quieting your voice. Even in silence, you can
offer yourself to another by opening your heart and soulfully
connecting to them.

I engage with others by opening
my heart and soulfully connecting
with them.

RAISE YOUR VIBRATION

"Blessing and releasing unhealthy relationships with unconditional love and integrity can teach us how to forgive our past, heal ourselves, and generate positive energy to progress on our spiritual path."

– DR. DEBRA REBLE

Raise your energy vibration by opening your heart and radiating beams of love. Visualize this energy emanating from your heart center so that it fills the room. People emitting lower vibrations will rise to match higher vibration in your presence

This simple practice of putting your attention at your heart center and emitting love energy raises your vibration and the vibration of those around you. Love energy brings you into non-resonance with lower vibrations, and you can still radiate love from a distance without losing yourself.

By raising my vibration, I raise the vibration of others and send this energy out into the world.

YOU HAVE PERMISSION

*"Appreciation can make a day, even change a life.
Your willingness to put it into words is all that is necessary."*

– MARGARET COUSINS

When you follow your heart, you live with passion and purpose. Following your heart is key to nurturing your creativity, fostering your spiritual growth, and living in alignment with your soul's path

Give yourself permission to follow your heart in some new way. Let go of something that no longer inspires you, and choose something more appropriate to your current life. When you enjoy doing something that you put your heart and soul into, love and joy follow.

When I follow my heart, I live a life
of purpose and passion.

GRACEFUL TRANSITIONS

*"Leaving a legacy of love is the path of seeing life as a challenge,
an adventure and, most of all, a gift."*

– DR. DEBRA REBLE

Move through any transition in your life with ease and grace. View transitions as times of gathering strength physically, mentally, and spiritually in preparation for your next step forward in life, just like springing up at the end of a diving board to gather momentum for a full twist into the pool.

Although moving through any transition may make you feel that you are losing your bearings, they are spiritual signs that you are downloading new spiritual information to expand the course of your life.

I move through any transition
with ease and grace.

SOULFUL ALIGNMENT

"What really counts during a time of transition is remembering that YOU are at the wheel for how you cope with it... happiness starts with YOU!"

– JESSICA DUGAS

Living a soul-hearted life takes discernment and the strength to stand in your truth. This means seeing who or what is enhancing positivity and who or what is bringing negativity into your life.

Consider what soulfully aligns with you, and what does not. Choose what sustains your well-being and the well-being of the planet and all its inhabitants. Listen to your heart and allow spirit to guide you. If anyone or anything does not feel aligned with your highest self, trust your intuition, and change the situation as soon as possible.

I discern what brings positivity into my life and what brings negativity.

YOUR SOUL POTENTIAL

"Trust yourself, listen to your heart, and use your expanded conscious awareness to guide you on your journey."

– DR. DEBRA REBLE

When you emanate love, you ascend to the highest level of your soul. You perform better at work, are more creative, healthier, and positively impact your world. You become a change agent of love.

To transform the planet, you are called to activate the soul potential within you to co-create a new world of love. To discover your soul potential, you have to trust yourself and courageously excavate all that inhibits your full self-expression.

By emanating love, I ascend
to the level of my soul.

HONOR YOUR INNER GODDESS

*"In every given moment we have a divine spiritual
assignment in front of us: Choose love or choose fear."*

– GABRIELLE BERNSTEIN

Embrace your exquisite feminine body with all of its flaws and
imperfections. Look in the mirror, connect to your feminine
energy, and accept your body without reservation. Revise any
shame messages that lead to embarrassment or self-consciousness
and change them to love messages. Honor, appreciate, and cherish
your sacred body by giving it the love and precious care it needs.

Connect to your inner goddess and express your sensuality and
sexuality without inhibition. Be fully present in your body and
feel the vibration of your divine feminine energy when you
channel it through sex, yoga, dance, or movement of any kind.

I embrace my divine feminine
body and express my sensuality
without inhibition.

FEEL TO HEAL

"Living a soul-hearted life requires radical acceptance: acceptance of ourselves, others, and our current circumstances."

– DR. DEBRA REBLE

Notice when you feel anxious, restless, or irritable. Lean into these feelings instead of ignoring or avoiding them. These emotional cues are part of your spiritual guidance system and alert you to any unhealed part of yourself so that you can feel and heal it.

Sit compassionately with your emotional pain until it releases and dissolves into self-love. When you trust yourself enough to let go, your courage kicks in, enabling you to see that your emotional pain is no match for the energy of love within you.

I allow my emotions to surface so I can feel and heal them with love.

SOUL GAZING

*"Creating a home that nourishes and supports
your whole being is one of the most important actions
that you can take for yourself today!"*

– FELICIA D'HAITI

By inviting love in and connecting with someone on a soul level,
you grow spiritually. The relationship becomes a portal that
allows both of you to become more loving and compassionate
human beings. Loving and connected relationships lead to a more
loving and connected world.

Practice "soul gazing" with your friend, family member, or
partner. Face them, take a few deep breaths, gently cradle their
hands, and lovingly gaze into their eyes. Open and connect heart
to heart in silence. Experience the love, inner peace, and spiritual
attunement with them. Appreciate them for who they are.

When I gaze into my loved one's
eyes, I connect with their soul.

BE A ROLE MODEL OF SELF-LOVE

"Love must be the motivation for everything we think, say, and do."

– DR. DEBRA REBLE

Children look to their parents and caregivers to mirror the love that they are. If you want your children to feel loved and worthy, you need to treat your home as a safe sanctuary. Create a climate of love, an energetically safe space where they can fully express themselves and feel lovable just the way they are.

Be a role model of self-love for your children. They develop self-love by being surrounded by people who are loving, caring, and fully accepting of themselves and others. By feeling worthy and lovable, you reflect to your children that they are worthy and lovable. Creating a climate of love takes becoming a champion of self-love.

I walk my talk of self-love
and worthiness.

SOUL ELEMENTS

"The question isn't who's going to let me; it's who is going to stop me."

– AYN RAND

When your life feels out of balance, you can feel unsettled, ungrounded, and question who you are and what you really want. This is a divine sign that it's time to shift your priorities and reflect on what's aligned with your soul. If you have defined yourself by your job, achievements, or relationships, it is time to discover who you truly are at the soul level.

Journal your core values or soul elements—these are what you hold dear, the aspects of your life that matter most, and the non-negotiables in your life. Then ask yourself, "Am I directing most of my time and energy here?" Strive for emotional and spiritual balance by allocating more of your time, energy, and resources to what is core to your soul.

I reflect on what is core to my
soul and direct more of my time
and energy there.

A COSMIC NUDGE

*"Trust isn't developed in one full sweep; but rather
in practicing small leaps of trust one moment, experience,
or situation at a time."*

– DR. DEBRA REBLE

You don't think or feel your way into being courageous, you take inspired action. Having courage of heart allows you to break old patterns, clear your fear, and make inspired choices to co-create your reality.

Courage is a cosmic nudge that takes you out of your comfort zone and into your power center. It gives you the power to embrace your truth, step out of the shadows, and shine your light. Every time you courageously lead with your heart, you become the person you are soulfully meant to be. It is saying a resounding "Yes" to what the universe has in store for you.

I courageously lead with my heart
and say yes to the universe.

REWRITE YOUR STORY

*"Dance with your soul's light, allow yourself
to show up to live your life fully with your contribution
to humanity. The world needs you."*

– ANNA-CHARLOTTE HANDLER

When you are fully present, you show up with your entire being. You experience an overwhelming sense of joy and contentment. There is no aching, yearning, or dissatisfaction to distract you from what is happening in the present moment.

Refrain from creating stories about your past and simply be in your present experience. Like a ball of yarn, it can be tempting to wrap strand after strand of stories about the past. You may think that these stories represent you; yet, they only bring your past into the present. Rewrite your story, shift your perspective from the past to the present, and see the magnificent being you are now.

I release my past narrative and
see myself from the perspective
of the present.

FREE FROM THE PAST

"Flexibility is a hallmark of lightheartedness which leads to a life with ease and grace."

– DR. DEBRA REBLE

Forgiveness is an act of love in which you focus your energy through your heart center, and bless and release anything that does not align with who you truly are. Forgiveness promotes well-being because it encourages the release of negative emotions, such as anger, resentment, or a desire for revenge.

Forgiveness frees you from the past and severs the flow of negative energy toward others so positive energy is returned to you. The simple act of blessing and releasing any person or situation creates space in your heart to love and be loved and moves you forward on your spiritual path.

I bless and release anyone or anything that blocks the flow of love through my heart.

POSITIVE AND PEACEFUL

*"You're being called to shine your light and transform
the world with your sacred gifts. Embrace your light!"*

– LINDA JOY

By loving yourself, you send ripples of love to others and into the
world. Your higher vibration elevates the vibration of the world,
so it becomes a more positive and peaceful place. To create
positive energy, you don't have to sit cross-legged on the floor for
hours, chanting positive mantras. You can create positive energy
simply by radiating love energy from your heart, one beam at a time.

Your light and love, when directed positively, will bring about a
greater good, peace, and harmony to all human beings. It is this
love force that is bringing about the transformation you are now
experiencing in the world.

I radiate love energy from my heart
one beam at a time.

TRANSCEND NEGATIVITY

"Healing the wounded child takes making a commitment to one's transformation, and is a challenging, yet, courageous venture."

– DR. DEBRA REBLE

Practicing compassionate detachment gives you the power to transcend any negative person or situation with care. Like operating the zoom lens of a camera, detachment allows you to pull back, creating the healthy distance you need. When you zoom out, you gain a more spiritually elevated perspective. This gives you the capacity to feel compassion for even those who deceive or hurt you.

Open your heart and surround that person or situation with light and love. This will elevate your energy and release any residual negative energy. Strive to view any "negative nellies" as catalysts for you to ascend to a higher level of awareness.

I compassionately detach from any negative situation.

MIND THE GAP

*"To create a major change in your life, start choosing
what you really want. Don't let current circumstances, the past,
or other people choose it for you."*

– ANN SANFELIPPO

Become more mindful of your thoughts and feelings by
practicing mindfulness movement. One way to do this is by
taking your mind, body, and spirit for a walk. Start by going
outside for a fifteen-minute walk. Do so without your phone or
music as a distraction. Before you begin your walk, stand on the
earth and draw your attention down into your feet.

As you walk, notice your breath. Shift your focus to your steps
and notice how your body feels as you move one step in front of
the other. Observe yourself taking a step forward toward your
future, and then releasing your back foot, letting go of your past.
The space between your steps is the present. Be mindful of this
space as you walk.

I practice mindfulness
movement when I walk.

TAP INTO NATURE'S GIFTS

*"Responding rather than reacting to life helps us
to make more enlightened choices."*

– DR. DEBRA REBLE

Nature grounds, balances, and energizes you. Spending time outdoors, walking through the woods, or just communing with nature brings you into the present moment. Through nature, you experience an inner connectedness with all living things. Feeling this sense of divine connection can be a lifeline during times of distress and despair.

Take time each day to go outdoors to elevate your mood, balance your energies, and ground yourself. Go barefoot in the grass, lean up against a tree, or float in a pool or lake to calm and restore your energies.

I use the elements of nature to
calm and energize me.

MAKING EMPOWERED CHOICES

*"Love and the power of courage hold no boundaries.
Embrace your passions and inner wisdom to guide you
to your soul's purpose."*

– TARAH ABRAM

Choice is a powerful tool when you are accountable for your life. Start by sitting quietly, opening your heart, and asking yourself these questions when making any choice, "Does this choice align with my soul's path? Does this choice bring me inner peace? Does this choice create joy and well-being? Does this choice enhance my life?"

Listen to your heart and answer these questions truthfully. You will always be guided in whatever direction is right for you. Then make the inspired choice and handle whatever comes from it positively.

When I listen to my heart, I make
the best choices possible.

HONORING YOUR ENERGY

"Co-creating the life we want begins with us. If we each take responsibility for the energy we project by becoming more conscious of our intentions, thoughts, feelings, and choices, it will be possible to transform our lives and our world."

– DR. DEBRA REBLE

If you are a highly sensitive person, you may feel deeply, care too much, and are overly empathic. Because you take in the negative energies of others, you may feel anxious or empathy overload. This energetic drain can make you vulnerable to compassion fatigue.

It is essential that you consistently create healthy boundaries and discern what emotions and energies are yours and which ones are not. Be discriminating of the people, situations, and environments that are not conducive to your sensitivities and spend as little time as possible there.

I choose to spend time with people who elevate my energy.

IGNITE A RIPPLE OF LOVE

"Loved ones leave us in the flesh, but their mark remains indelible on the soul. Revel in the gift of love, miss with full feeling, and be completely grateful."

– JAMI HEARN

Your soul is calling you to step into your power as a woman, matriarch, and spiritual midwife. Women, as an energy source, must take the lead to transform the consciousness of the world to one of love, harmony, and peace. You have been preparing to be a feminine leader all your life and are ready. Be courageous, fearless, and shine your light so that others can shine their lights as well.

Create a legacy of love through your children, grandchildren, partner, friends, and anyone you serve. Channel love and create what you want in alignment with what is best for yourself, others, and the world. Let your legacy ignite a ripple of love that transforms others and the world.

I create a legacy of love that
transforms others and the world.

LANGUAGE OF LOVE

"When we can rise above whatever is happening in our lives, we increase our compassion for others."

– DR. DEBRA REBLE

Sharing a language of love connects you, heart and soul, with another person. It is a way to engage in open and honest communication and heighten intimacy in your relationship. It only takes an open heart, love-light in your eyes, and nurturing words to create a soulful connection with someone.

Embrace compassionate communication. Rather than saying, "Leave me alone," which can feel harsh and dismissive, you can say to someone, "Please let me be." This phrase lets the other person know in a loving way that you would like some personal space. Similarly, instead of telling someone you don't like them, communicate to them that their behavior is unacceptable or hurts your feelings.

When I communicate compassionately, it opens intimacy and connection with others.

FEEDBACK FROM THE UNIVERSE

*"Surrender is flowing with the magical unfolding of life,
in complete trust and knowing, all are here to serve me
and bring me my highest good."*

– LIZETE MORAIS

Trust that your spirit is stronger than any problem you can possibly face. Embrace every situation not as a source of fear, but as an opportunity for spiritual growth. Focus on the light in these dark moments of the soul, and affirm your inner strength in handling whatever comes your way.

Instead of saying, "Why did this happen to me," ask yourself, "What is this challenging person or situation revealing to me about myself??" Accept what's in front of you, even when it's difficult. Welcome this spiritual feedback from the universe and incorporate it into your daily life.

I embrace the feedback the universe
gives me to guide my life.

VIBRATIONAL DETOX

"When you tap into your spiritual resilience, you gain the perspective to accept any situation, no matter how difficult or painful, as an opportunity for personal transformation."

– DR. DEBRA REBLE

After any negative encounter or situation, it is essential that you detox from the lower vibrational energies you have absorbed. Taking deep cleansing breaths, bathing or showering, and spending time in nature are ways to clear your energy field and restore balance.

When you are ready to share anything that may be toxic, be considerate of your friend or partner by asking if it is a good time to vent. This gives them time to energetically prepare for having the conversation so they won't absorb any residual negative energy.

I clear my energy field of any
negative energy through self-care.

PHOENIX RISING

*"When each of us as women fully embodies the frequency
of our sacred worth, we blaze a trail for future generations
who walk in our footsteps."*

– MARCIA MARINER

Alchemy is burning away the "dross" of an ordinary material and transforming it into a refined substance such as gold. When you render any material, you strip away the layers, exposing what's underneath. Spiritual alchemy is the process you go through when you strip away your physical patterns exposing the refined essence of your soul—your true being.

You spend the first part of your life acquiring layers of patterns from your childhood experiences. Then, you spend the second part of your life releasing these layers that no longer serve you. Love transmutes whatever it touches into its highest potential. Like the phoenix rising from the ashes, this transmutation reveals the essence of your soul as love.

I transmute the layers of my patterns
revealing my true being.

YOU ARE LIMITLESS

"There came a time when the risk to remain tight in the bud was more painful than the risk it took to blossom."

– ANAIS NIN

Your future is a blank slate upon which you can inscribe your unique imprint from an unlimited palette of choices. Let go of any self-imposed barriers and realize that there is nothing you cannot create, express, or experience. Discover a newfound awareness of how limitless you truly are.

With this sense of spiritual freedom, realize the fullest extent of your imagination. See that the possibilities are endless and choose from among them. Embark upon a new journey by traveling, taking a class, making a new friend, or engaging in a new experience.

I let go of any self-imposed limits and feel free to create new experiences.

BEAUTY AND WONDER

*"When we break free of our comfort zones and surrender
our resistance and control, we tap into an unlimited source of positive
energy and creativity and begin to see our experiences
from an expanded perspective."*

— DR. DEBRA REBLE

Living in the flow of love, you are fully present and notice the
beauty and wonder in the world around you. You tune in to your
senses, which turns up the volume on the artistry that surrounds
you. With this heightened awareness, you create experiences of
awe, wonder, and a sense of connectedness.

Be more mindful of your wonderful world and savor your
experiences. Gaze up at the stars, listen to the sound of a wind
chime, or feel the rain on your face. Watch nature unfold in its
brilliance and see the parallel in your own life.

When I live in the flow of love, I am
more present to the beauty that
surrounds me.

NEW BEGINNINGS

"It's like a muscle: the more you use your body's wisdom to make decisions, the easier it becomes."

– PAMELA THOMPSON

Letting go is all about the completion of life cycles. Such completion signals a beginning more than an ending. Realize that you are part of these natural cycles of life and death. Death is not something to fear because you can view death as simply one more transition—like moving from one room to another.

Let go of the current form of your life so it can transform into a new one. Embrace such experiential death, not as an upset, but as an essential part of your spiritual progression. With these heightened spiritual energies, remain grounded as everything changes around you.

I embrace letting go as a new beginning rather than an ending.

SEEK THE LIGHT WITHIN

*"When a woman conceives her true self, a miracle occurs
and life around her begins again."*

– MARIANNE WILLIAMSON

It's not always easy to sustain a positive attitude or outlook on
life. But, even in the darkest moments, seek the light, blessing,
or spiritual information in every situation. Trust that you are
stronger than any situation, and with every challenge comes an
opportunity to grow spiritually.

Express lightness and the joy of living so that you manifest
wellness. Trust yourself, celebrate being, and love more. Be
spontaneous, throw caution to the wind, and choose consciously.

In my darkest moments,
I seek the light within.

SPIRITUAL SUPPORT TEAM

*"When you truly know that you can trust yourself,
you can reflect that energy into the universe and attract
the people you want in your life."*

– MICHELE GREER

Relationships provide you with numerous opportunities for
self-realization and to spiritually progress beyond what you can
achieve alone. Examine your current relationships to see who
supports your spiritual growth at this time.

Ask yourself, "What unresolved issues are my relationships
showing me about myself? Do my relationships support me in
my spiritual growth? Are they assisting me to be the best I can
be?" Journal your answers.

I examine my relationships to see
who supports me on my path of
spiritual growth.

THE GIFT OF ANXIETY

"Miracles are instantaneous—they cannot be summoned,
but come of themselves, usually at unlikely moments
and to those who least expect them."

– KATHERINE ANNE PORTER

Anxiety lets you know that there is information you need to pay attention to and act upon. Your anxiety signals where there are energy blocks (physical or emotional pain) in your body, mind, and spirit. Whenever there are energy blocks in your body, and especially when those blocks are produced by excessive negative thoughts, you become prone to physical or emotional dis-ease.

Anxiety gives you the heads up on what unresolved issues need to be healed and what feelings need to be released. This healing can lead to positive transformation and, ultimately, making healthy life changes.

I pay attention to any anxiety and act
on the information it gives me.

DEVOTE TIME TO YOURSELF

The most important relationship you have in your life is with yourself. Yet, so often it gets placed on the back burner. You may lose yourself in relationships by setting aside your own needs for those of others even when it compromises your health and well-being.

Know that you are a loveable and worthwhile being, apart from your partner or children. Cultivate a relationship with yourself at a deeper, more spiritual level. You cannot create healthy, soul-hearted partnerships until you first cultivate a healthy partnership with yourself.

I devote time and energy
to cultivating a healthy relationship
with myself.

TRANSFORMING LOSS

There is no preparation you can undertake for the life-shattering loss of a loved one. It is an unfathomable pain that penetrates your life and pierces your heart. However, you can choose to honor your soul connection with your loved one by transforming your loss into love. You can channel the energy released at your loved one's death by putting their powerful light to positive use.

Direct the energy of your loss by sending love out into the world for the betterment of humanity. Become a more kind and compassionate partner, patient and tolerant parent, and supportive friend and co-worker. Channel your loss into love by healing others as you rid the world of racism, abuse, and hatred. Resonating as a field of love, you can become a love activist in this love-starved world.

I transform my loss into love.

SPEAK YOUR INTENTIONS

*"Listening to our body, not our mind, is the path to
ensuring the choices we make honor our spiritual, mental,
and physical well-being."*

– MICHELLE LEMOI

Any thought or spoken word functions as an intention so keep your
thoughts and words positive. Your words must source from the
energy of love. The phrase "be careful what you wish for" applies to
the potential outcomes of thinking or speaking negatively.

If you catch yourself thinking or speaking negatively, shift your
intention, words, or tone to be more positive. The high vibration
of positive words has an uplifting effect on your life, whereas the
vibration of negative words has the power to damage or destroy.

I choose my words positively
to reflect the intentions I want
to create.

MEMO FROM THE UNIVERSE

"Self-care is giving the world the best of you,
instead of what's left of you."

– KATIE REED

You are always moving through transitions. You move from winter to spring, darkness to light, and from germinating to blossoming. Like change, transitions are constant and cyclical. Transitions, when used wisely, are powerful. Your intentions set in motion these transformational shifts and it is up to you to make the best use of this creational space.

These are the times when you know your memo to the universe has been heard, and everything feels like it's in commotion or co-motion. Trust what is in store for you and your future and move through these times with ease and grace.

I move through transitions
with ease and grace.

AVOID AND RELEASE HOOKS

"No one is you, and that is your superpower."

– ELYSE SANTILLI

The best way to detach from people who engage in negative patterns is to disengage from the "hook" of these patterns. To avoid these hooks, you need to be aware of the source of any vulnerabilities and take note of the people and situations that push your emotional buttons and trigger your reactions.

Then release your vulnerabilities privately, or with a trusted friend before re-exposing yourself to another sensitive situation. Another way stay responsive is to write down your feelings in a journal until you feel a cleansing or release of emotion.

I recognize the people and situations that push my buttons, and I disengage from the hooks of their patterns.

MIRACLE MOMENTS

"Dare to turn the doorknob of success and step into the life you've always dreamed of! Become a spectacular talent acknowledged repeatedly!"

– KATHLEEN GUBITOSI, MA

Miracles are those moments that dramatically alter your perspective, open you to divine intervention, and manifest something beyond what you ever thought possible. They are initiated by co-creation with your source and can take you beyond thought, belief, and any physical condition.

Notice the miracles all around you, not just the grand "Aha" ones. Sometimes the smaller miracles help you see divine intervention even more than the big ones. Above all, you always receive what you need to heal and see your divine truth. See the message in the miracle.

I make choices that invite in miracles.

KINDRED SPIRITS

"Take up more space, everywhere. Spread out like a starfish in the middle of your bed. Expand beyond your comfort zones. Grow. Challenge. Thrive."

– DEBORAH KEVIN

Select an energetic support team comprised of soul-hearted friends and partners who encourage your spiritual growth. Be sure that the people you gather around you show up when you need them and support your well-being. These kindred spirits hold up a mirror so that you can see your beautiful being.

Fine tune your soul team by periodically adding or letting go of people in keeping with your spiritual progression. Let go of the people who drag you down and choose the people who lift you up. Surround yourself with people who have your back, as well as your heart.

I choose relationships that reflect back to me the truth of who I am.

OPEN TO TRANSFORMATION

*"I am guided by the wisdom of my inner light. I am a
woman, a sacred container, whole and beautiful.
I am perfect in my imperfections."*

– CRYSTAL COCKERHAM

You may feel an expansiveness of energy nudging you to release
your fear and step into your soul's purpose. With spiritual
expansiveness comes the release of any constriction in your body,
mind, and life where there are energy blocks. This signals that you
are opening to transformation and it is worthwhile.

Bring awareness to the places in your body where you feel any
energy blocks. Direct loving energy from your heart to these
tender places that hold fear or unhealed wounds. Focus your
attention here until you feel the energy surface and then release.
Ask yourself: "What fear or trauma am I releasing? What is the
spiritual message for me?"

When I expand spiritually,
I release any energy blocks in my
body, mind, and life.

SEEDS OF INTENTION

"Instead of waiting to see if you measure up, start letting everyone else know that they don't have to."

– MELISSA CAMARA WILKINS

Declare your intentions clearly. Select words or phrases that represent your intention, write them on Post-It notes, and put them wherever you will notice them. Each time you see your intention, put a white light around it, and affirm it to yourself.

Close your eyes and imagine that your intention has already manifested. How does this look and feel like in your life? See yourself abundant and powerful. Plant the seeds of your intention and, when given the opportunity, make the inspired choices that will manifest it.

Every choice I make, I make with clear intention.

THE VOICE OF YOUR SPIRIT

"The power is in the asking!"

– ROBBIE MOTTER

When you tune in and listen to spirit, you gain a broader perspective on your life. Listening to spirit is like listening to an imaginary best friend. With practice, you can discern the voice of your spirit through physical sensations, a feeling of intuition, or an image that pops into your mind. You have tuned into spirit when you have said, "I can sense it in my body, I can feel it in my bones, or the answer is right on the tip of my tongue."

You can hear the voice of your spirit more clearly while listening to music, writing, or exercising. It doesn't matter how the information comes through you; what matters is when you receive it, you trust it to guide your life.

I listen to my spirit to receive
information to guide my life.

WALK IN GRACE

*"Without leaps of imagination, or dreaming,
we lose the excitement of possibilities. Dreaming, after all,
is a form of planning."*

– GLORIA STEINEM

Soul-hearted partnership opens up opportunities for you to walk in grace every day. When you and your partner pursue a path of spiritual growth, you commit to being the best you can be. Rooted in heart and soul, you support each other to live fully realized.

Soul-hearted partnership shows you that you can be alone together. In this sacred journey of relationship, both partners are committed to supporting the well-being of each other as well as the relationship itself. With this comes a deepening intimacy, passion, and support of your own and your partner's spiritual progression.

As a soul-hearted partner,
I support and am supported
to live fully realized.

BALANCED CAREGIVING

"Just don't give up trying to do what you really want to do.
Where there is love and inspiration, I don't
think you can go wrong."

– ELLA FITZGERALD

Practicing balanced caregiving can be a challenge. As a woman, it is your nature to nurture, care, and serve the needs of others. But, you may put the needs of everyone else first at the cost of yourself. You may think that you have to do it all, do it perfectly, and never let anyone see you sweat. This caretaking pattern can lead to an imbalance in your body, mind, and life.

You are here to love, be love, and to serve; but, your service must be a balanced exchange of energy. Practice balanced caregiving by putting your needs first so you can then assist others. Be in the service of yourself as well as those you love.

When I practice balanced caregiving,
I put my own needs first so
I can assist others.

SUPPORTIVE LISTENING

"Success is getting what you want,
happiness is wanting what you get."

– INGRID BERGMAN

Open compassionate communication by asking your friend
or partner if you have the "permission to speak freely" about
a situation that has been troubling you. Clear announcements
of your expectations can open the way for supportive listening
and empathy.

Practice giving and receiving feedback. Start by focusing on
minor issues and progress to major ones. Use statements such
as, "Are you open right now to feedback? May I suggest? or Do
I have permission to speak freely?" If it becomes difficult for
your friend or partner to continue listening, pause and table the
discussion until later. Resume when you are both calm and ready
to listen.

I compassionately communicate in an
open and non-judgmental way.

EMBRACE YOUR SOUL POWER

"We must let go of any expectations of how life SHOULD be,
in order to experience how life CAN be."

– DR. DEBRA REBLE

When you hide in the shadows, you miss the opportunity to fulfill your dreams. To claim your authentic power, you have to uproot the patterns and mindsets that have formed your false "safe zones." It's time to let go of fear and put your heart and soul out there.

Release any resistance and embrace your future. Take a leap of trust so you can fulfill your soul purpose. By saying yes to new opportunities, you are saying yes to yourself. Yes, you are accountable for your life. Yes, you will embrace your soul power. And yes, you will step out of the shadows and into your light.

I step out of the shadows and into my light to create my dreams.

ENERGETIC INTEGRATION

*"The art of manifesting miracles is to open our hearts, our beliefs
and our lives wide enough— to actually receive the magic
and miracle by grace."*

– LIZETE MORAIS

It's essential to integrate your male and female energies, so you
co-create healthy and balanced relationships. The flow of energy,
which channels through soul-hearted relationships, transcends male
or female, becoming greater than the energy of the two individuals.
Each partner functions as a complete power source and contributes
one hundred percent of this energy to the relationship.

This energetic dynamic can occur in all types of relationships
in which individuals have a soul connection with each other.
When you operate as the source of love, you make choices
that are not bound by gender. As a result, this flow of energy
keeps expanding in all aspects of your life until your whole life
experience becomes soul-hearted.

I integrate my male and female
energies to create soul-hearted
relationships.

FREE FROM COMPARISON

"When we unearth our sacred gifts and cultivate them, our divine destiny and prosperity are without a doubt being accomplished."

– MARCIA MARINER

Feel secure in your own life without the need for comparison or judgment. Free yourself from the opinions and expectations of others. Refrain from comparing yourself to others or their circumstances that keep you doubting and defending yourself. Feelings that surface when you compare yourself with others are a barometer of how much you love yourself.

When someone says, "I love my life," feel happy for them. Then affirm to yourself, "I love my life, too." When you love yourself, you do not envy the good fortune of others. Instead, trust that there is enough love, success, and abundance to go around.

I let go of comparing myself to others and trust that there is more than enough to go around.

CREATING MY HAPPINESS

"Within each of us is a divine universe of love."

– DR. DEBRA REBLE

You may feel that the pursuit of happiness is elusive or unattainable. You may think that if you had the right job, relationship, or money that you would be happy. However, happiness is a state of being—well-being that is within your grasp. You have always had the power within you to create it.

Choosing happiness is experiencing a homecoming to your heart. To be truly happy, you must wholeheartedly love yourself. Rather than looking backward, regretting what might have been, choose to look forward through the lens of love. Discover that you are not only worthy of love but love itself.

I sustain a positive flow of energy which creates my happiness and well-being.

YOUR SOUL'S PROGRESSION

*"Many persons have a wrong idea of what constitutes
true happiness. It is not attained through self-gratification
but through fidelity to a worthy purpose."*

– HELEN KELLER

Soul mates appear in your life to support your soul's progression.
They enhance your life by providing insights, unconditional love,
and assistance with life's challenges. These relationships often
meet a need or fulfill an intention that you have expressed. They
also come to assist you with difficult situations and provide you
with guidance and support.

You attract such soul-connected people into your life by being
your own soul mate, committed to doing the spiritual work it
takes to stay true to your soul's journey.

I attract soul mates into my life to
assist with my soul's progression.

CALL OF YOUR SOUL

"Use compassionate, empowering words when talking to and about yourself—you are listening and will script your story according to your own narrations."

– DR. COLLEEN GEORGES

Transcend fear by allowing things to be without resisting or avoiding change. Clear your fear and let go of all you hold onto from the past. Anything from your past can create an energy block that interferes with your health and well-being.

When you no longer hold on to anything, you give yourself the freedom to follow your heart. Move through your day without trying to force anything to happen. Create positive intentions and trust your spirit to guide your choices.

When my soul calls,
I take time to listen.

EMBRACE CHANGE

"Her inner fire edged out like a sword sweet and free,
it stretched from the inside into the outside world
ebbing and flowing with light."

– HEATHER MARIA

Move with the constant flow of change no matter what it
may look like, when it may happen, or where it may take you.
Transformation calls for you to step outside of your own little
world, realize the bigger picture in front of you, and make a
conscious shift in your life that is always for the better.

You are being challenged to let go of excess, to right size, and
simplify your life. Examine your life and become aware of how
you are using your energies. Question who you are and what you
truly want. Dig deep and ask yourself these life questions,
"Why am I here? What is my life's purpose? How will I live?"

I go with the constant flow of change.

LOVE YOUR IMPERFECTIONS

"Each person's soul journey is unique yet dependent on the genuine love, support, and connection with others."

– DR. DEBRA REBLE

Embrace your imperfections, make mistakes, and create messes.It's okay to struggle or have a challenging day. But, when life comes at you and you feel discouraged, love and accept yourself in the midst of the messiness. Pause and check in with yourself so you know whether you have moved out of the higher vibration of love and into fear. If so, drop into your heart space, be conscious of your thoughts, and shift them from fear to love.

Through the eyes in your heart, see your imperfections in a new light. Instead of feeling ashamed, fully accept them and let them show you who you are at your core. Embrace all parts of your beautiful being.

I embrace my imperfections
with love and acceptance.

DIVINE VALIDATION LIST

*"When we are present in our bodies, we inhabit
the present moment, we are not lamenting the past
or worrying about the future."*

– DR. CATHERINE HAYES, CPCC

You may feel discouraged at the slowness with which you realize
your dreams. Be mindful it's always about divine timing, not time.
When you trust divine timing, you realize that things go more
smoothly than you could ever imagine. Let go of impatience, declare
your intentions, and allow the universe to co-create with you.

Create a divine validation list in your journal. Every time you get
a divine sign from the universe that supports your intention or
gives you the guidance you need, write it down. Then when you
doubt yourself or feel uncertain, review your list. This will open
your awareness to the divine signs that are always around you.

I let go of impatience and
trust divine timing.

MAKE PLAYFUL CHOICES

*"Connect with your soul and your truth, go with the flow
and let everything fall into place, acting on what feels right.
Believe and trust in yourself!"*

– KRIS GROTH

Live fully and fearlessly by experiencing your spirit at play. Look at life through the lens of your inner child with awe, wonder, and delight. Notice the ordinary things that make life extraordinary.

Play opens sacred space to connect with your divine energy. Expect nothing and invite in everything. Experience the freedom to channel your energies to create beyond any limitation. Embody the mantras of "What's next? and Let's see."

I open my spirit to play.

IT STARTS WITH GRATITUDE

*"The gift of no: release the need to always say 'yes,'
and know that you offer an opportunity by allowing
the person to step into their divine power."*

– CAROLYN MCGEE

A gratitude practice shifts your mindset from scarcity to prosperity. Acknowledge the blessings you already have in your life, even if you do not necessarily feel this way. Start with feeling blessed for being alive, followed by other blessings in your life. This will generate more positive energy and multiply exponentially when your intentions are aligned for a greater good.

Acknowledge the blessings of who you are and what you already have, Repeat the mantra,"I am a blessed being," or "I bless myself, my fellow human beings, and the earth no matter what." Prosperity is the result of giving and receiving in love. It's not something you acquire or hold onto, but rather a flow of energy you emit through your heart.

I am grateful for all the
blessings in my life.

PERMISSION GRANTED

*"There is no growth without risk. It is like taking
a walk on the beach in a thunderstorm. Lightning turns
sand into beautiful beach glass!"*

– AMY JOHNSON

The spiritual principle of "permission" sets you free to make
enlightened choices for your well-being. There is no need to
validate your choices through outside sources such as your boss,
friends, or even your partner. Instead, give yourself permission to
play with all the possibilities and fully express who you are.

Don't let your "to do" list overwhelm your life. Create a "to be"
list that encompasses the experiences that bring you joy and allow
you to follow your heart. When you want to try a new experience,
say to yourself, I give myself permission to _____.

I give myself permission to just be.

GO WITH THE FLOW

"Bright and burning; filled with
potential—give your love; it's exponential!"

– SUSAN KAY DAHL

When you sustain a positive flow of energy, you hold steady in the midst of the natural twists and turns of life. There will always be circumstances that challenge you in ways beyond what you think you are capable. These moments are divine opportunities to transform your life.

This is when you need to let go of your expectations and "go with the flow." By trusting yourself and your inner power, you remain open to this positive flow of energy and move through any challenge with grace, ease, and responsiveness.

I am capable of handling any challenges with ease, grace, and responsiveness.

BREATHE AND LET IT BE

"If your actions create a legacy that inspires others to dream more, learn more, do more and become more, then, you are an excellent leader."

– DOLLY PARTON

Release any fear about your life not going as planned. Trust yourself and your source for co-creating the life experience unfolding in front of you even if it is not the one you expected. Just as a plane is guided into the air, you, as a co-pilot with your source, are guiding your intentions into reality. With trust, let go of any expectation, outcome, or plan.

Dissolve past patterns, beliefs, and mindsets so that any negative energy can be released and new positive outcomes can emerge. Align with this shift by allowing things to be as they are for a while without fighting, fleeing, or flailing. Breathe and let it all be.

I trust the divine unfolding
of my life even if it doesn't go
the way I expected.

MOVING PAST YOUR FEARS

*"Measuring up to some imaginary standard of perfection
is not necessary. We're all beautifully imperfect."*

– GENEVIEVE KOHN

When you confront the source of your fear, you discover that the person or situation that seems terrifying in your mind is not at all what you thought it to be. Fear often becomes amplified in your mind and can easily paralyze you.

It takes courage and compassion to dig deep and face your fear. Sit and lean into your fear like a long lost friend and have a sacred chat with it. When you trust yourself as a source of genuine power, your innate strength and courage kicks in and moves you past whatever you fear most.

I lean in, dig deep, and have
a sacred chat with my fear.

LISTEN TO SPIRIT

"When we break free of our comfort zones, we no longer feel we have to sacrifice our worthiness. We let go of our fixations with what other people think, and show up fully."

– DR. DEBRA REBLE

Be still enough to hear the whisper of spirit through your heart. Your spirit will remind you of who you are and what your heart most desires. The more you open your heart and access this guidance, the more you expand your perspective on life.

Close your eyes, open your heart, and trust the spiritual information that comes through you as a divine download. Listening to spirit allows you to consciously override the mental chatter of your brain that may overwhelm you. Listen to your spirit and follow your heart's desires.

When I listen to spirit,
I follow my heart.

YOUR SPIRITUAL SUPERPOWER

"Don't let anyone rob you of your imagination, your creativity, or your curiosity. It's your place in the world; it's your life. Go on and do all you can with it and make it the life you want to live."

– MAE C. JEMISON

The space of vulnerability is the pathway to an authentic life. Vulnerability is a spiritual superpower that allows you to show up fully in your life. Facing your deepest vulnerabilities helps you to recognize and uproot the negative beliefs and unhealthy patterns that inhibit you from living an abundant, joyful, and balanced life.

Remember, that the stronger your reaction, the more deeply seated your vulnerability is to that particular pattern, person, or situation. Just becoming aware of your vulnerabilities can unblock your energy, freeing this energy to create what you truly want in your life.

When I react strongly, I need to become aware of the root of my reaction.

SHIFT YOUR REALITY

"Breathe in the understanding that you have the right to be happy. Each day you can set powerful intentions to make the most of your life."

– FELICIA BAUCOM

No matter how challenging your circumstances, you can shift your reality through the power of intention. When you view life through the lens of a positive mindset, you have more possibilities in life than you could possibly envision.

Every experience you have reflects your intention. When you react negatively to someone or something, you generate more negativity, while your positive responses produce more positivity. With your power of intention, trust your ability to make your dreams come true.

I shift my reality through
the power of my intention.

CHOOSING INNER PEACE

*"Your external world is your playground; it wasn't meant
to be a measuring stick for your worth."*

– EMILY MADILL

Reflect on a situation where you were faced with a challenge, obstacle, or difficulty. What was your predominant mindset? Did you react from your headspace, "Why did this happen to me?" Or did you respond from your heart space, 'What is this situation revealing to me about myself?"

If you reacted by blaming or judging, you reinforced a negative mindset. This negativity feeds anxiety. Yet, if you responded with trust that everything would be okay, you strengthened a positive mindset. Whether you react (negative) or respond (positive) to the events that happen determine a life of anxiety or peace.

When I view the events that
happen with a positive mindset,
I create a peaceful life.

NATURE'S HEALING ENERGY

"Spiritual growth requires us to take responsibility for the patterns, beliefs, and choices we make in our lives, and compassionately eliminate all that is not in alignment with our soul's journey."

– DR. DEBRA REBLE

Make time to go outside today even if it is for just a few minutes. It can boost your mood, expand your creativity, and even improve your memory. Head outside for at least twenty minutes of fresh air. Use this natural anti-depressant to open your heart and lift your spirit.

Pause today and take time to notice, sense, and let nature's beauty wash all over you. Let it fill you up with its potent life force energy. Reflect on the transitory nature of life itself, so you are inspired to make the most of this day.

I take time outside and let nature's life force energy fill me up.

RESCRIPT YOUR ANXIETY

*"I have learned over the years that when one's mind
is made up, this diminishes fear; knowing what must
be done does away with fear."*

– ROSA PARKS

You may have negative, anxiety-inducing scripts playing in your head. It's time to rescript your anxious thoughts into empowering affirmations. Positive affirmations can move you from fear to inner peace. They help relieve anxiety, calm the nervous system, and elevate your vibration to a higher level. With mindfulness, you can learn to shift your thoughts and the anxieties they trigger.

Write down in your journal your predominant anxiety-inducing scripts. Then next to each script, write a positive affirmation. For example, if one of your scripts is, "I never have enough money," you can rewrite the script into an affirmation such as, "I am connected to the unlimited abundance of the universe."

I use positive affirmations to
alleviate my anxiety.

INTO THE SPACE OF TRUST

"Self-care is not a luxury. It's a non-negotiable necessity."

– KELLY MISHELL

Trust is the energetic space between your fear and everything working out well. Imagine crossing a deep chasm with no bridge to get to the other side. The side you are standing on is fear and on the other side is what you want to create in your life. When you step into thin air, you are stepping into the space of trust.

Trust isn't tangible, but an energy that you feel when you let go of fear. By being bold-hearted, you co-create the invisible trust bridge that takes you to the other side of fear. This level of absolute trust is the greatest gift you can give yourself.

When I let go of fear, I step
into the space of trust.

AN ILLUMINATED PATH

"You are more powerful than you know;
you are beautiful just as you are"

– MELISSA ETHERIDGE

Life presents you with the opportunities to find peace in turmoil. In such moments when faced with an unexpected situation, you can feel anxious, unprepared, and even a sense of futility. But, with any challenge comes an opening, a beginning, and a transformational path that is illuminated.

When you tune in to your heart, you access the seat of your soul. Acknowledge yourself as a strong, loving, and intuitive woman connected to your divine source. This perspective will help you view any life experience as a divine opportunity to transform your life.

My challenges are divine opportunities to transform my life.

EMBRACE WHAT IS

*"The brilliance of the star is her ability to connect with
another person in this great big world."*

– MARIE MARTIN

Let go of any expectations that impede the positive flow of
energy in your life. Expectations of yourself, others, or any
situation are your greatest obstacles to living in the flow of love.
When you become attached to a particular outcome, you set
yourself up for stress and disappointment.

Embrace any experience that comes your way and allow it to
unfold. Celebrate the day no matter if the lines are long, or the
wait time more than you realize. Enjoy these experiences by
sustaining humor, flexibility, and a sense of adventure.

I let go of any expectations, allow
what is, and embrace whatever
comes my way.

LOVE AND CONNECTION

"It's all about showing up!"

– ROBBIE MOTTER

Acknowledging your need for love and connection is the first step in discovering your essence as love. Being and expressing love in connection with others is your divine legacy and your soul purpose for being here. You need to belong, to connect, to love, and be loved.

Widen your circle of loving compassion to all living beings. Inviting in love and connection with others creates a world of peace and compassion. Loving and connected relationships lead to a loving and connected world.

I am soul-wired for love
and connection.

MANIFEST YOUR DREAMS

*"Desire is the seed planted for cultivating our new reality.
Vision is the water, sunlight, and air that gives
our desire what it needs to grow."*

– ANN SANFELIPPO

Making your dreams a reality is a divine gift as well as your responsibility. In co-creating with your divine source, you can consciously choose what you want in your life. Not honoring your heart can stifle the creation of new possibilities.

All it takes to spark co-creation is one pearl of light, the seed of possibility. With this, you can channel your energy to manifest your dreams from an array of infinite possibilities. Answer this call to co-creation.

I co-create with my divine source
to make my dreams come true.

LISTEN WITH COMPASSION

*"The power you have is to be the best version of yourself
you can be, so you can create a better world."*

– ASHLEY RICKARDS

Create a safe environment to have a heart-to-heart talk with a
friend or partner. In this sacred space, listen compassionately to
the other person without judgment or interruption, and be open
to supportive feedback. Don't take anything personally, make
assumptions, or draw conclusions.

Enhance this feeling of safety by sharing your feelings honestly
using phrases such as, "I feel," instead of "You make me feel."
Throughout the conversation, accept each other's feelings as real,
valuable, and meaningful.

I create a safe space for having an
honest heart-to-heart conversation
with another person.

PERMISSION TO GRIEVE

"When love is flowing through us, we are powerful to envision and create whatever our heart desires."

– DR. DEBRA REBLE

It is critical that you mourn the significant losses in your life. Without grieving, you cannot fully release the feelings that continue to weigh heavily on your heart. Remaining stuck in the grieving process leads to a state of unremitting grief which clings to feelings of sorrow, anger, and depression.

When the pain becomes too much to bear, release it into the wellspring of divine love. In the midst of profound loss, your pain can be transformed into love. Share and express your pain and give it a sacred space to heal so you can become whole again. Let it be a spiritual springboard for action to assist others with loving-kindness.

I allow myself to grieve
and release the pain that weighs
heavily on my heart.

UNTAPPED SOUL POTENTIAL

"I can't think of any better representation of beauty than someone who is unafraid to be herself."

– EMMA STONE

You are part of a vast expanse of illuminating energy. This energy moves through space, is pulled into a field called gravity, and attracts matter. Such an energetic attraction becomes thought, which informs the body, and then information, which guides you to think, speak, feel, and act. This is the direct link to your soul.

Channeled through you, this energy transforms you into a creational being, capable of co-creating your reality. Realize that you have an infinite amount of creational energy to share and an untapped soul potential to manifest whatever you need or desire.

I have infinite creational energy
to manifest what I need or desire.

EMBRACE CHANGE

"Rather than trying to "shrink" ourselves so we continue to fit into a life that is too small or no longer serves us, midlife calls us to embrace the new direction our soul is urging us toward, and make the choice not to shrink, but to stretch."

– CHRISTY WHITMAN

When you are in the midst of change, be grateful, graceful, and grounded. Clear your life of any unhealthy relationships, environments, or choices that no longer serve you. Sustain a lightness of being through breaking old patterns and aligning your energies with new intentions.

Release the negative patterns that no longer serve you and expose more of your true being. This process leads to a new beginning and a spiritual awakening. Trust the voice of spirit to guide you in completing and forgiving the past.

I embrace change as it clears the way for my spiritual awakening.

UNSHAKABLE JOY

*"We call in grace when we surrender control and allow
our lives to unfold into the present moment."*

– KRISTINE CARLSON

Real unshakeable joy comes from any transformational
experience that sources from deep within your soul, takes your
breath away, and brings you to your knees. Align with what
awakens your soul, and you will sustain joy in your life.

Exuding positive energy is a magnet for creating joy. Live in
an open and lighthearted way. Be playful and willing to try
something new or something you have always wanted to do.
Make a joy list and then do the things on the list with creative
abandon. Take life less seriously, and see it as a passionate
adventure to be enjoyed.

When I align with what awakens
my soul, I live joyfully.

SEEK CREATIVE OUTLETS

*"Have a rock star professional life and still maintain time
for divine self-care. Follow your inner voice—NOT the one
telling you anything else."*

– JAMI HEARN

Creative work cannot exist without play. Seek creative outlets to
channel the energy that is released when your heart is open and
your spirit playful. When you are creatively inspired, you can
override the chatter of the brain and tap into your heart and soul.

Never be intimidated by your creative expression. Write, dance,
or sing to direct the flow of your energies creatively. Be receptive
to creative experiences that encourage you to explore outside
your comfort zone. Share a creative idea or project with a friend
or colleague.

I unleash my unlimited
creative power when I tap into
my heart and soul.

THE POWER OF YOUR WORDS

*"I've learned from experience that the greater part of
our happiness or misery depends on our dispositions
and not on our circumstances."*

– MARTHA WASHINGTON

When you change your thoughts, words, and actions, you change your life. See yourself as a powerful energy source and abandon any self-defeating roles you play in the world. Listen to your highest self and no longer follow anyone else's direction, belief system, or idea of who you should be.

Speak your truth even when you are afraid of what others may think. Find the inner strength to show up and be fully seen and heard. Trust and follow the calling of your heart and soul. Become the person you are meant to be by saying "YES" to the universe.

When I change my thoughts,
words, and actions, I change my
life and the world.

THE WINDOW OF AWARENESS

"When we shift our perception and release the old stories we transform and our hearts open to endless possibilities of imagination and creation."

– TARAH ABRAM

You are born to be an open channel of spiritual information, for it is your divine nature. You can use both hindsight and insight to gain foresight, the ability to envision the future results of your choices. Tapping into your foresight allows you to bypass moments, months, or even years of life's lessons.

Through this window of awareness, you can see that it is no longer valuable to trudge through the pain and drama of life's lessons. With foresight, you can become more present, proactive, and make the inspired choices that prevent lessons.

I am proactive when I use foresight
to guide my choices.

HOLDING SACRED SPACE

"All of us are born with the ability to be an open channel
of spiritual information, for it is our divine nature. Take time
to tap into this channel daily."

– DR. DEBRA REBLE

Sometimes to assist someone you love, you need to step into
a situation that is immersed with pain and sadness. You are
called to hold sacred space for healing. Being fully present with
someone's vulnerable pain creates a sacred space where they can
be completely seen and heard.

The word "scared" becomes "sacred" by interchanging two
letters. It is the space of unconditional love that heals pain and
suffering. Holding the space of love for someone to heal their
heart is the greatest gift you can give them.

I create sacred space for
someone by offering my divine
presence of love.

BE THE LIGHT

"We can change our view of change by viewing the uncomfortable moments as an opportunity for tremendous transformation."

– ARIANE DE BONVOISIN

Travel as an ambassador of love by respecting the inherent worth in everyone and interacting compassionately with those you meet. When you travel as a love ambassador, you open your heart, share love, and be the light. Shining your light is fully expressing your highest and best self through your thoughts, words, and actions.

You can be a beacon of hope and reflect the light that you see in others. In a world that desperately needs it, you can sow seeds of love wherever you go, leaving it a better place for having been there. Be the light and see the light in others.

I am light and see the light in others.

YOUR FULLEST EXPRESSION

*"When you get under the spout where the glory comes out,
you will soak up enough light to be a beacon for others."*

– SUSAN KAY DAHL

Your greatest challenge is to accept your extraordinary power as love and channel it to make the world a better place. To do this, you must shift from an ego-driven life to a soul-given one. If you are to assist in transforming the world to one of peace and harmony, you must recognize that you are your own power source.

Your true power originates from within and initiates your reality. As a co-creator, you can wield this power to make soul-hearted rather than self-centered choices. Trust your connection to your divine source and channel it to support the fullest expression of yourself, others, and your world.

When I tap into my true power as love, I make soul-hearted choices.

THE MAGIC IN THE MESSINESS

"The moment when you believe that you are the star of your story is the moment you stop letting the other characters define your role."

– MICHELE GREER

Pay tribute to the sacredness of life. Be present and notice the magic even in the messiness. Life doesn't always turn out the way you think it should; yet, you can choose to focus on the blessings rather than the burdens. When you view your life through the lens of your heart, you will see the sacredness of it all.

Gaze up at the stars, wash the dishes, connect to a loved one, and be reverent of your wonderful world. See the sacredness in everything around you. Make your life a series of sacred, perfect miracles.

I choose to make my life a series of miracles by focusing on the sacred.

SHIFT YOUR THOUGHTS

*"You may have to lose who you were to find out the
sacredness of who you truly are and want to be on
your magical journey!"*

– CINDY HIVELY

When you feel hesitant, uncertain, or anxious, you need
"encouragers" to tap into courage and build confidence. Positive
affirmations strengthen your courage and confidence especially
when you feel fear, doubt, or powerlessness. When you shift your
fear-based thoughts to positive ones, you drop into your heart
space which elevates your energy field from fear to courage.

As you go through your day, notice any self-limiting thoughts and
replace them with positive affirmations. You become free of your
fear-based thoughts and self-sabotaging behaviors by opening
your heart in courage and confidence.

When I open my heart, I access the
courage and confidence that
is always there.

LOVING RELEASE

"We cannot change what we are not aware of, and once we are aware, we cannot help but change."

– SHERYL SANDBERG

When both people take responsibility for letting go of their relationship, they validate the purpose the relationship has served and their experiences in it. Acknowledge the intention that brought you together and lovingly release the relationship with respect, care, and appreciation.

Although it may be tempting to cut and run, it is beneficial to allow time for a healthy and healing break up before you move on to someone else. You need to spiritually complete the relationship to clear the space for co-creating a new one.

I spiritually complete any relationship before beginning a new one.

RELEASE EXPECTATIONS

"Our beautiful female bodies are soul instruments,
finely tuned to give us messages to become more aware.
Dare to listen and go deeper."

– ANNA-CHARLOTTE HANDLER

Celebrate the holidays without expectations. Let go of trying to please everyone and choose what brings you joy. Give yourself permission to break with tradition. Be open to creating new experiences and allow unexpected miracles to unfold.

Take a vacation, try a new holiday activity, and spend more relaxed time with yourself and loved ones. Release any fear of the holiday being less than perfect and trust that it will unfold as it is meant to be. Create the holidays as a time of beauty, quiet reflection, and a celebration of love.

I celebrate the holidays with no expectations, allowing the unexpected miracles of the season to unfold.

ACCEPTING ALL PARTS

"To manifest magic and miracles in our life, we truly need to be in alignment with what our soul knows is ours."

– LIZETE MORAIS

Realizing that you are worthy of love begins with connecting with the unloved parts of yourself. You have always had the power within you to heal your lovelessness. Yet, before you can heal, before you can fully love and connect to yourself, you need to accept your imperfect parts.

Accepting yourself as whole and complete requires spending time alone so you can confront the source of your feelings of unworthiness. Be compassionate company with yourself, as if you are with an old, trusted friend. Write a love letter to your inner little girl telling her she is loved and loveable just the way she is.

There is nothing I need to do to establish my worth.

CELEBRATE THE LIGHT

"As we peel away layers of the past, we develop a spiritual clarity that transforms our history and opens us to possibilities."

– DR. DEBRA REBLE

The winter solstice celebrates the return of the light and is a time of quiet reflection and intention. As soon as the first star is out, take time to reflect on the things you want to let go of this year and the things you want to bring into your life. Write down the people, situations, and patterns that you are ready to release and forgive. You can put these slips of paper in the fire or shred them.

Now focus your intentions on what you want to bring in to your life. Sit quietly, open your heart, and meditate on your intentions. If you feel inclined, write them down in your journal or put them in a special box to reflect upon later. Trust that you will manifest an abundance of all that is good, loving, and joyful in your life.

I reflect on what I want to let go of and what I want to bring into my life.

YOUR TRUE ENERGY SOURCE

"I've learned that you shouldn't go through life with a catcher's mitt on both hands; you need to be able to throw something back."

– MAYA ANGELOU

The strongest electromagnetic field of energy in the human body emanates from the heart. When fully opened, your heart center creates an energetic vibration that illuminates the surrounding space. This is your unique energetic signature, and it impacts everyone and everything around you.

Love is in every atom of your being. When you operate as a source of love, you generate high vibrational energy that brings your body, mind, and spirit into harmonic resonance. Tapping into this energy source, you create an expanded field of energy that interconnects you with all living things.

When I open my heart, I tap
into the strongest force of energy
in the universe.

EMBRACE UNCERTAINTIES

"Far away there in the sunshine are my highest aspirations. I may not reach them, but I can look up and see their beauty, believe in them, and try to follow where they lead."

– LOUISA MAY ALCOTT

There's always going to be uncertainty on the bumpy ride of life because change is constant. It's human nature to fear change, resist letting go, or want to stay in your comfort zones. Yet, absolute trust gives you the courage to embrace life with all its uncertainty.

So when faced with a difficult situation, you can choose to trust and start moving forward, or you can stay stuck in fear. The choice is yours. Even if you choose not to do anything, it is still a choice and a choice motivated from fear. Trust and let go. Become proactive and the co-creator of your life rather than the victim of your circumstances.

When I fear change, I make a choice so I can move forward.

TAKE THE LEAD

"Bring it on, revel in the strength that comes from adversity!
Resiliency makes us into women of courage, who then guide
and support others by example."

– MARGARET-MAGGIE HONNOLD

Women must take the lead to transform the world into one of love, harmony, and peace. Your service is greatly needed in creating a global initiative of love for humanity. You can model for others that the power of love transcends gender, culture, race, and religion. Above all, every person is one in the energy of love.

As a conscious evolutionary of love, you can harness that power and demonstrate that anything is possible. This high vibration of love creates a more positive and peaceful planet.

Through my high vibration,
I elevate the consciousness of
the world to love.

LOVE AND PEACE

*"Trusting ourselves and letting go is the
ultimate courageous act, and also the most powerful
and inspired action we can take."*

– DR. DEBRA REBLE

Hearing a favorite song, experiencing a child's embrace, or seeing the sun setting over the horizon opens your heart and touches your soul. When you hear a favorite song, you may feel transported to another place and time. When you cannot contain the love that overflows your heart, you are filled with joy.

When your heart is wide open, you may feel like a sunburst opening, with waves of warm energy vibrating within the center of your chest. With this energetic expansion comes a sense of love, peace, and spiritual awakening.

When love overflows my heart,
I am filled with joy.

FEED YOUR SOUL

*"Great minds discuss ideas, average minds discuss events,
small minds discuss people."*

– ELEANOR ROOSEVELT

Love compassionately. Trust yourself. Let go of fear. Practice loving-kindness. Speak your truth. Forgive often and quickly. Bless and release your past. Embrace your vulnerabilities. Do what makes your heart sing. Open to gratitude and grace. Live and serve with love. Lead with your heart. Create space for healing. Celebrate your blessings. Make love to life. Be gentle with yourself. Shine your light. Feed your soul. Be courageous.

I illuminate the light
that shines within.

THE VOICE OF YOUR HEART

*"The more you nurture yourself, the more you
value yourself, and the more you value yourself,
the more you prioritize nurturing yourself."*

– KELLEY GRIMES, MSW

Choose which voice to listen to, the voice in your head (fear) or
the voice in your heart (trust). When faced with a situation that
triggers fear ask, "Are going to listen to the voice in your heart or
the voice in your head?"

You can't choose whether to feel fear, but you can choose what
to do with those thoughts and feelings when they come up. This
is where you have control. No matter how powerful your fear is,
you can choose to focus on your heart and listen to your inner
voice. Trust is a real and powerful energy that lives in your heart
and is always a part of your present awareness.

I choose to listen to the
voice of my heart.

RELEASE EMOTIONAL RESIDUE

*"When we get quiet, soften our heart and make peace
with our current condition, we avail ourselves to divine guidance.
From here, change is inevitable."*

– LISA HINTON

Along with releasing emotional residue, let go of any physical
residue from a past relationship. Because the physical residue
of the relationship may still be lurking in your environment,
consciously check your surroundings for any items that may be
holding past energy.

If you open a drawer and see papers, photos, or gifts from
a previous relationship, regard it as a sign to keep what you
cherish and discard the rest. Once you have finished, journal the
answers to these questions, "Where in your life do you still have
unfinished relationship business? How does this person's memory
still hold you back? What do you still need to release and
forgive completely?"

I clear the physical and emotional
residue of past relationships.

COMPASSIONATE CONNECTION

"Don't compromise yourself. You are all you've got."

– JANIS JOPLIN

Kindness and compassion generate a high vibrational energy field that supports forgiveness. Practice radiating compassion to another person from your heart. Seeing this person in love brings you into grace, where you can accept what is and forgive what isn't.

While sitting quietly, place your hand on your heart and visualize a pearl of white light in the center of your chest. Allow your light to expand outward as a radiant cord of light, connecting your heart with the person you want to forgive. Direct love toward them and feel the expansiveness of the energy flow as it comes back to you through your heart.

When I compassionately connect heart-to-heart with someone, I open to forgiveness.

EMBRACE YOUR SHADOWS

"As we are liberated from our own fear, our presence automatically liberates others."

– MARIANNE WILLIAMSON

When your light is brightest, you see your shadowy parts the clearest. Your patterns of overcompensating, overachieving, and people-pleasing only keep your fear of inadequacy in the dark. Let down your guard by removing your ego-clad armor and open and embrace your shadows.

The foundation for cultivating a loving relationship with yourself is accepting all of you, even the shadowy parts.

When my shadows are revealed,
I embrace the truth of who I am.

MUSTER THE COURAGE

"The stars are here to remind us we are all meant to shine!"

– TARAH ABRAM

Muster the courage to face your fear of being visible. Step out of your comfort zone and into your stretch zone. In these soul-stretching moments, take a few deep breaths, open your heart, and embrace your truth. Clear any self-doubt and insecurity by reminding yourself, "I've got this."

Be courageous and express your authentic self. Drop your masks, let go of any facades, and allow yourself to be seen. Like stepping stones across a stream, authenticity comes from making a series of small, impeccable, heart-aligned choices every day.

I step out of my comfort zone to be soulfully seen and heard.

NEW YEAR INTENTIONS

"Wake up in the morning and acknowledge yourself as a strong, loving, and confident woman connected to your divine source."

– DR. DEBRA REBLE

As you end this year, spend time in solitude to create your intentions for the New Year. Reflect on what you are letting go of from this year and what you want to bring in next year. It is also a time to energetically complete any spiritual ties or unresolved issues.

Invite in blessings and let go of disappointments. Resolve to complete this year with love, forgiveness, and gratitude for everything that has brought you to this moment. This aligns with your soul's journey and empowers you to be a force of light, love, and all that is good. Be the light in the world that you came here to be.

I spiritually complete this year with love, light, and gratitude.

SACRED CONTRIBUTORS

Tarah Abram, Bestselling Author and Coach
www.JuicyLivingbyDesign.com

Felicia Baucom, Transformational Coach
www.FeliciaBaucom.com

Charlotte Bifulco, Tutor Cleveland Heights, OH

Tonia Browne, Heal Your Life® Workshop Leader and Coach
www.ToniaBrowne.com

Deb "GypsyOwl" Bryan, Creative Time Today
www.GypsyOwlWire.com

Carmella Calta, Chagrin Falls, OH

Laura P. Clark, Master Soul Coaching® Practitioner and Instructor
www.SoulWiseLiving.com

Crystal Cockerham, Energy Alchemist
www.WisdomAwakens.com

Lorene Collier, Personal Finance Coach
www.SavvyChicksRule.com

Susan Kay Dahl, Creator of Honest Answers
www.SusanKayDahl.com

Michelle Deeb, School Psychologist
www.laasponline.wildapricot.org

Felicia D'Haiti, Feng Shui and Soul Coach®
www.FeliciaDHaiti.com

Mal Duane CPC, CRC, Midlife Transformation Coach
www.MalDuaneCoach.com

Jessica Dugas, Intuitive Mentor
www.JessicaDugas.com

Joyce Fennell, Health and Wellness Practitioner
www.SanctuaryByJoyce.com

Dr. Colleen Georges, Positive Psychology Coach
www.ColleenGeorges.com

Elaine Gibson, The Healthy Lifestyle Designer
www.RenewedLivingInc.com

Michele Greer, Transformational & Lifestyle Coach
www.MicheleGreer.com

Kelley Grimes, MSW, Counselor, Author, Speaker
www.CultivatingPeaceAndJoy.com

Kris Groth, Spiritual Mentor & Energy Healer
www.KrisGroth.com

Kathleen Gubitosi, MA, Holistic Voice Strategist
www.KathleenGubitosi.com

Anna-Charlotte Handler, Transformational Life Coach
www.Thrive-TLC.com

Dr. Catherine Hayes, CPCC, Inspirational Speaker and Bestselling Author
www.CatherineHayesCoaching.com

Jami Hearn, Intuitive Prosperity Coach
www.JamiHearn.com

Lisa Hinton, Change Coach
www.LisaHinton.com

Cindy Hively, Intuitive Healing Coach
www.InHerFullness.com

Ann Marie Hoff, Intuitive Medium, Inspirational Speaker,
Animal Communicator, and Artist
www.AnnHoff.com

Margaret-Maggie Honnold, Registered Nurse, Health Educator,
and Author
www.MargaretHonnold.com

Susan Wilking Horan, Attorney, Three-Time Cancer Survivor,
and Wellness Advocate
www.SusanWilkingHoran.com

Amy Johnson, Soul-Hearted Human Being, Bay Village, OH

Linda Joy, Visibility Catalyst and Bestselling Publisher
www.Linda-Joy.com

Deborah Kevin, Writer, Editor, and Storyteller
www.DeborahKevin.com

Genevieve Kohn, Abundance Creation Guide
www.GenevieveKohn.com

Bonnie Larson, Healing Minister
www.FlyingSoHigh.com

Michelle Lemoi, Transformational Life and Business Coach
www.YourPartnerInGrowth.com

Michelle Lewis, aka The Blessings Butterfly, and Inspirational Speaker
www.TheBlessingsButterfly.com

JoAnne B. Lussier, Reiki Master Teacher
www.TheWillowConnection.com

Emily Madill, Author and Coach (ACC)
www.EmilyMadill.com

Heather Maria, Spiritual Advisor
www.HeatherMaria123.com

Marcia Mariner, Sacred Wealth Coach
www.MarciaMariner.com

Marie Martin, Inner Beauty Cultivator
www.CandidAndClassy.com

Carolyn McGee, Intuition Empowerment Guide - Healing Through The Heart
www.CarolynMcGee.com

Kelly Mishell, Certified Law of Attraction Life Coach
www.KellyMishell.com

Lizete Morais, Life Transformational and Personal Development Coach
www.AuthenticVoice.co

Robbie Motter, NAFE Global Coordinator/GSFE CEO
www.RobbieMotter.com

Nettie Owens, Productivity and Accountability Consultant
www.MomentumAccountability.com

Gwendolyn M. Plano, Author
www.GwenPlano.com

Lore Raymond, Author, Writing, and Creativity Coach
www.LoreRaymond.com

Ceri Ridenour, Soul Care Ministry
www.SoulLettersWellnessCare.com

Isabella Rose, Holistic Health Practitioner
www.BellaRoseHealingHands.com

Debbie Sain-Bissette, Sunset Beach, NC

Ann Sanfelippo, Wealth Coach
www.WealthAttractionAcademy.com

Yaelle Schwarcz, Soul Artist and Guide
www.SowingTheWildSeeds.com

Pamela Thompson, Transitions Coach
www.Pamela-Thompson.com

Katt Tozier, Resilience Expert
www.MysticKatt.com

Liliana Vanasco, Women's Empowerment Mentor
www.LilianaVanasco.com

Cornelia Ward, Divine Career and Business Coach
www.IHelpPeopleLoveMondays.com

ABOUT THE AUTHOR

Dr. Debra Reble

Consciously merging her practical tools as a psychologist with her intuitive and spiritual gifts, **Dr. Debra L. Reble** empowers women to connect with their hearts and live authentically through her transformational Soul-Hearted Living™ teachings, speaking, and intimate retreats. She is also the creator of the popular AnxietyRXProgram.com.

Debra is the author of the international best-seller, *Being Love: How Loving Yourself Creates Ripples of Transformation in Your Relationships and the World*, as well as *Soul-Hearted Partnership: The Ultimate Experience of Love, Passion, and Intimacy*, which garnered four book awards including the Eric Hoffer award. A frequent guest contributor to *Aspire Magazine* and other high-profile blogs, as well as a sought-after speaker and guest on podcasts and summits, her words of wisdom are embraced by women around the world.

Her popular inspirational podcast, *Soul-Hearted Living*, airs on iTunes and other platforms and is dedicated to reconnecting women with their hearts.

She is also a contributing author to the international bestsellers, *Shine: Stories to Inspire You to Dream Big, Fear Less & Blaze Your Own Trail, Inspiration for a Women's Soul: Choosing Happiness, Inspiration for a Woman's Soul: Cultivating Joy, Inspiration for a Woman's Soul: Opening to Gratitude & Grace, Midlife Transformation: Redefining Life, Love, Health and Success*, and *Courageous Hearts: Soul-Nourishing Stories to Inspire You to Embrace Your Fears and Follow Your Dreams*, all published by Inspired Living Publishing, LLC.

Debra has a thriving private practice in Cleveland Heights, Ohio, and also sees clients virtually. She has two amazing children, Tom and Alex, and lives with her beloved husband, Doug, and yellow Labrador, Shiloh. She loves to travel, cook, practice yoga, and dance tango and salsa with her husband.

Visit www.DrDebraReble.com to discover inspiring content and supportive resources.

ABOUT THE PUBLISHER

Founded in 2010 by Inspirational Catalyst, radio show host, and *Aspire Magazine* Publisher Linda Joy, Inspired Living Publishing (ILP) is an international best-selling inspirational boutique publishing company dedicated to spreading a message of love, positivity, feminine wisdom, and self-empowerment to women of all ages, backgrounds, and life paths. Linda's multimedia brands reach over 44,000 subscribers and a social media community of over 24,000 women.

Through our highly-successful anthology division, we have brought eight books and over 300 visionary female authors to best- seller status. Our powerful, high-visibility publishing, marketing, and list-building packages have brought these authors—all visionary entrepreneurs, coaches, therapists, and health practitioners—the positive, dynamic exposure they need to attract their ideal audience and thrive in their businesses.

Inspired Living Publishing also publishes single-author books by visionary female authors whose messages are aligned with Linda's philosophy of authenticity, empowerment, and personal transformation.

Recent best-selling releases include *Everything Is Going to Be Okay: From the Projects to Harvard to Freedom* by Dr. Catherine Hayes, CPCC; *Awakening to Life: Your Sacred Guide to Consciously Creating a Life of Purpose, Magic, and Miracles* by Patricia Young; the award-winning *Being Love: How Loving Yourself Creates Ripples of Transformation in Your Relationships and the World*, by Dr. Debra L. Reble; and the multiple award-winning *The Art of Inspiration: An Editor's Guide to Writing Powerful, Effective Inspirational & Personal Development Books*, by ILP Chief Editor Bryna Haynes.
ILP's family of authors reap the benefits of being a part of a sacred family of inspirational multimedia brands which deliver

the best in transformational and empowering content across a wide range of platforms.

Our hybrid publishing packages and à la carte marketing and media packages provide visionary female authors with access to our proven best-seller model and high-profile multimedia exposure across all of Linda's imprints (including *Aspire Magazine*, the "Inspired Conversations" radio show on OMTimes Radio, the Inspired Living Giveaway, Inspired Living Secrets, and exposure to Linda's loyal personal audience of over 44,000 women.)

If you're ready to publish your transformational book, or share your story in one of ours, we invite you to join us! Learn more about our publishing services at **InspiredLivingPublishing.com**.